For: Margie and Harold

From: Anne and Al

COOKING
ON
THE
GO

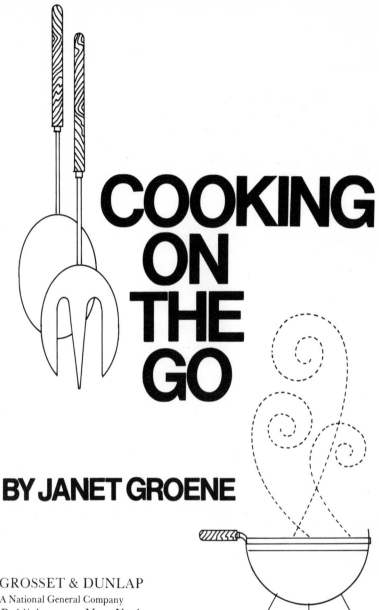

COOKING ON THE GO

BY JANET GROENE

GROSSET & DUNLAP
A National General Company
Publishers   *New York*

Special Thanks

To the international fraternity of fellow fly-swatting, wave-wallowing, smoke-choked, chigger-scratching wanderers who make up the campsites and docks, and who shared their favorite recipes for this book.

Printed in the United States of America

To M. and D.
who honeymooned in a tent
and lived happily ever after

CONTENTS

INTRODUCTION

To some campers and boaters, like the family we once saw in a Michigan state park eating canned spaghetti from paper plates, outdoor adventure means an escape from kitchen chores. For others more fortunate, a go-away galley is as elaborate as a kitchen at home, complete with ovens and gas burners, freezers and blenders, air conditioning and ice makers.

Many of us, though, prefer to camp or sail simply. Still, we want meals that are attractive, nourishing, and varied. Camping in our Volkswagen Microbus, we cooked only over open wood fires and sometimes spent hours gathering wood, simmering steamy iron pots, and washing up afterwards in buckets of fire-heated water. To us, this was part of the sport of camping.

Now, in our 30-foot sailboat, we have a two-burner Primus stove with no oven, refrigeration that works only if we are plugged into dockside electrical power (which isn't often), a tiny, single-faucet sink, and a work area no larger than a card table. Yet we regularly have home-baked bread, cakes and pies, hot meals from real dishes, and substitute salads served days away from port.

This book is for the distance sailor and the wilderness camper, who refuse to be dependent upon electricity, gas and water, doorstep milk and newspapers, and fresh supermarket produce. Today, far from the city, we are eating better than ever before.

JANET GROENE

SHOPPING FOR YOUR TRIP

How many of us are organized enough to plan menus months in advance and buy food for them? Not I! Besides, you never know when you'll stumble on a patch of ripe berries in the woods, a catch of fish in a stream, or a find of crawfish in a coral shoal. But there are certain general requirements you'll want to remember, as a back-up to fresh meat and produce that you'll be able to catch, trade for, or buy along your route.

For two, I plan a pint of meat (or can of tuna or tin of corned beef, etc.) for each day we will be gone. To this, add one can of vegetables per day, buying a good balance of green and yellow vegetables and a variety of beets, canned squash, onions in jars, and red cabbage. In your count of vegetables don't include starchy courses like potatoes, baked beans, or the canned tomatoes you will use in cooking. One tin of fruit per day seems about right, too.

After these have been stored, you can fill your canned goods lockers with such extras as tinned soups, pickles and olives, and various trims and special garnishes.

You know from the rate you consume it at home how much instant coffee to buy. For the two of us, both using creamer in our coffee, we use about three jars of powdered cream to two jars of instant coffee. Plan about a half cup of flour per person per day; more if you eat bread, biscuits or pancakes for all three meals. Sugar use will be almost as much, especially if you use sugar in coffee and cereal.

I also keep in mind the number of days in our trip when I shop for lunchtime choices like small tins of liverwurst, packaged soups and cheese. You probably won't need a separate lunch plan for each day, though, because there will be leftovers from dinner sometimes. Our stretchable standby is peanut butter and jelly. We seem to average two jars of jelly for each jar of peanut butter.

Make a basic spice shelf of those seasonings you use most, and assemble such staples as baking powder, baking soda, packaged yeast, salt and pepper, cornstarch. I always carry instant-blending flour in the shaker package for sauces and gravies. Shop for dried parsley flakes, bacon bits, freeze-dried chives, instant onion, celery flakes, dried bell pepper, and other preserved condiments. Keep track of your family's milk intake, and then buy ahead in pre-measured quart packets.

After the staples are tucked away, it's just a matter of buying those items that you like most. Canned fruit juices and soda are bulky and heavy, but maybe dried drink mixes won't do for you. Peanuts and snacks will stay fresh in cans, and you'll want some if you're a family of snackers. Candy? Chewing gum? Cigarettes and liquor? Only you can plan them.

For instance, you can shop for a 30-day cruise or camping trip more easily in meal servings, than in a long list of individual items. For a family of four, list a four-serving can of meat as one meat "value," and plan one "value" for each family dinner. There will be times when you use more than a day's "value" because you are entertaining, and days when you don't use the alloted "value" at all because you have caught fresh fish or found a place to buy fresh meat.

Your shopping plan for a month's supplies might include:

30 main-dish meat values	
30 main-dish starch values	(Potatoes, rice, macaroni, spaghetti, sweet potatoes, baked beans, etc.)
30 main vegetable values	(Plan a good variety of green and yellow vegetables, plus beets, turnips, rutabagas, squash, and onions to be served as a vegetable. Buy some small-size cans for mixing, and any soups or sauce mixes you will serve with vegetables)
extra canned tomatoes for cooking extra onions for cooking	
30 fruit values	(Not counting breakfast juices; more than 30 if you eat fruit for both lunch and dinner)
30 breakfast values	(Will you need bacon every morning? Favorite cereals?)
30 lunch values	(Have on hand canned or dehydrated soups, bouillon, canned or unrefrigerated lunch meats and sausages, peanut butter, jams, cheeses in packages and jars)
30 Happy Hour values	(Popcorn, extra crackers, canned nuts and potato sticks, pickles, olives, drink mixes)
30 bread values	(Store bread will last a week, then use crackers, canned Bos-

	ton brown bread, homemade bread and biscuits, hardtack, etc.)
60 dessert values	(Some desserts will come from your fruit stock, but you'll need extra cookies for morning and midnight snacks. Plan desserts from recipes in this book; supplement them with packaged cookies, puddings, candy bars, fresh fruit)
½ cup flour per person per day (1 pound = 8 half-cups)	(You'll need far less, of course, if most of your baking is done from mixes)
Milk according to your family's needs 1 egg per person per day, if possible	

Staples

Coffee	Salt	Molasses
Tea	Pepper	Mustard
Baking powder	Shortening	Cornstarch or
Confectioners'	Granular yeast	instant-
sugar	Creamer	blending flour
Bouillon	Baking soda	Butter or
Ketchup	Vinegar	margarine
Sugar	Cooking oil	Jams
Baking choco-	Peanut butter	Cornmeal
late (or cocoa)	Flour	

Extras

Spices you use most	Bacon bits
Extracts (especially	Meat tenderizer
vanilla and maple	Condiments you use
flavoring for syrup)	most (Worcestershire,
Dried onion, parsley,	steak sauce, relish,
bell pepper	etc.)
Soy sauce	Mayonnaise or salad
Baking trims (Coco-	dressing
nut, nuts, chocolate	
chips)	

Instant breakfast mix
(Because this is a complete food,
you can use it for emergencies,
on hurried days, or when it is
too rough at sea to get a meal)

Freeze-dried chives,	Brown sugar
salad onions, mush-	Bottled lemon or lime
rooms	juice

Extend this list after reading recipes and choosing those that best suit your family.

STOWAGE

Your own sorting system will evolve after a few outings, to fit your own housekeeping style and available space. Because we have bilge stowage under our sloop's cabin sole, it is easiest for me to put canned meats in one compartment, vegetables in another, fruits in a third, lunch and snack cans in the fourth, fresh onions and potatoes in the fifth, and miscellaneous jars of olives, pickles, mustard, and the like in the last.

Dry mixes are kept together, and another locker is filled with frequently needed items—seasonings and spices, baking ingredients, coffee and tea, creamer, peanut butter, and jelly.

Hard-to-reach stowage spaces are not packed with similar items, however. I find it better to fill these bins and crannies with a selection of cans. Then, by emptying one out-of-the-way locker at a time, I can replenish each of the other compartments.

Some sailors prefer to pack their meals in plastic bags by the meal, the day, or the week. Robert Manry in his tiny *Tinkerbelle*, unpacked a week's supply of food at a time.

This system would also be best for a camper without an inside galley, to minimize the number of boxes that must be off-loaded to set up an outdoor kitchen. You might fill one hefty wooden box with dishes, silver, and pots; a second with every-meal items like salt, napkins, pepper, and butter; the next with a day's meals. Or, bring out a breakfast box for that meal, luncheon foods in a second storage box, and dinner ingredients in a third. You'll soon find out which system works best for you.

We learned the hard way that commercial packaging can't combat the kind of dampness that builds up in a boat or outdoor home, or the bugs that sometimes invade us. Even if your boat or camper is dry and without leaks, put crackers, cereals, cake mixes, and other dry foods that must keep for a long time, in plastic bags and seal with a rubber band or twist. Or, buy large plastic boxes that seal well, and fill them with dry foods. Plastic canisters are perfect for oatmeal, flour, sugar, cornmeal, and other staples, as well as crackers and cookies. Snap-lid coffee and shortening cans will work for a time too, although they rust eventually.

If your boat has a wet bilge, sea water will rust your canned goods overnight, and will eat through even aluminum cans in a short time. Remove all paper labels (paper will clog your bilge pump), and identify cans with a grease pencil. Then use rusted cans as soon as possible. To keep cans even longer, dip the entire tin, label and all, in molten paraffin. Work slowly and carefully over a very low fire. Paraffin will flare up if allowed to reach the smoking stage. Or you can seal cans very well in heavy plastic bags to prevent rust.

GALLEY GADGETRY

Take a long, careful look at every gadget in your utensil drawer at home before you award precious locker space to every gewgaw from your kitchen. The decision has to be yours, because only you know which utensils you use most for your own style of cooking, what grater works best for you, how much use you'll get out of a meat grinder or a gravy whisk.

For instance, I don't carry a potato masher because a slotted spoon (a wide one that I also use as a meat lifter) works to mash potatoes, sweet potatoes, or squash. Yet I can't part with my favorite peeler, although you might peel potatoes, apples, and carrots with a knife. Some people like a whisk for whipping, but I use a rotary beater. Your family may start every morning with poached eggs, but another crew would seldom use an egg poacher. A folding stove-top toaster could be a good investment for one family. Others can make do with a fork and an open flame, or biscuits instead of toast.

Take inventory of the utensils you use most at home. Then add to them the gadgets you will use more for camping or boating than you do at home. For example:

ice pick
hand can openers
"pinchers" for handling hot cans and jars
long-handled fork, spoon, pancake turner
asbestos shield to use over stove burners
small flexible frosting spatula (for removing cake
    from pan)
a selection of large shakers (to make eggs for
    scrambling, pancakes, nonfat dry milk)

Our only cooking utensils are:

heavy medium-size saucepan with lid
heavy skillet with domed lid

8-inch square cake pan
9 x 5 x 3-inch loaf pan
9-inch pie pan
4-quart pressure cooker
tea kettle

A typical menu, using only these pans, might start with a fruit cup. Then fresh tuna which has been baked in the heavy skillet, rice from the pressure cooker, carrots à l'orange from the saucepan, green beans heated in the can, biscuits or bread which have been baked ahead of time, and chocolate cream pie from the pie pan. We have served this meal, hot and for company, without even lighting our second burner! Water for instant coffee heats during dinner.

If you have room for nothing else, choose and carry a pressure cooker, even if you never use one at home. The locking lid makes it the safest pan you can use underway, and its shorter cooking time triples your fuel economy. On hot days, you'll bless the pressure cooker for reducing the time your stove runs, too!

This seems like a good place to mention our personal preference in stoves. After sampling cooking methods from open campfire to canned heat to homemade "buddy" burner to gasoline stove, we're still wildly enthused about our pressure kerosene stove. Sometimes hard to find in the States, they are made in Europe and are generally more expensive than American-made alcohol stoves. But we find that kerosene cooks with a hotter heat and lasts four and five times as long as the same tankful in an alcohol stove. Primed properly, and fueled with the proper, high-grade kerosene, these stoves have no kerosene smell and are completely safe.

Cruising the Bahamas, where alcohol for a stove costs an average family about four dollars a week, we meet many couples who have converted to kerosene by buying new burners in the Islands. By contrast, our kerosene cost isn't more than 7¢ a week even though I bake all our own breads and desserts. Alcohol, for priming, runs a few cents more per week.

DOWN WITH DISHWASHING!

It is always a virtue to keep dishwashing at a minimum. In water-shy wildernesses and on shipboard, it's a must. Still, paper plates aren't the pleasantest way to have dinner, and their cost adds up. And in a small boat like ours, it would be impossible to store enough paper utensils for a long cruise anyway! We compromise by having lunch, usually cold meats and crackers or sandwiches, from paper plates.

If you do dishes in sea water, you'll find that a dishwashing liquid suds well. Rinse thoroughly in plenty of salt water. Then, if you can spare the fresh water, rinse again, especially metalware. Glasses, if they aren't rinsed in fresh water, will have a cloudy look. Dry saltwater-washed dishes at once. And never buy kitchen utensils that will rust. It pays to buy stainless steel.

I manage to do dishes only once a day, by stacking dirty dishes in the dishpan, in a locker under the sink. But cooking and baking bowls are done instantly, wiped dry, and put away before dough has a chance to harden.

Paper cups in your galley can save you messy cleanups. Use them for mixing flour and water, or cornstarch and water, for sauces, and for serving gelatins and puddings. Although bathroom-size paper cups aren't substantial enough to hold liquids for long, they are handy for small herb mixtures or for blending cinnamon and sugar. I use them to hold garnishes for dinner dishes, and line them up to dash on just before serving, to avoid a last-minute scramble in lockers for parsley flakes, paprika, breadcrumbs, grated cheese, and other trimmings.

When mixing batters, or a dough that isn't too stiff, a plastic bag can save you from washing a mixing bowl. Line a bowl with the plastic bag (try several brands until you find the sturdiest), turning the top down around the edges of the bowl. Then put the ingredients in the bag, gather up the top in your left hand, and use your right hand to squeeze and knead the contents until batter is smooth. Squeeze it out into the baking pan, like toothpaste from a tube, throw away the plastic bag, and put your bowl away clean! If ground beef is soft and at room temperature, and if your plastic bags aren't the flimsiest kind, you can mix meatloaf this way too.

Don't skimp on plastic bags in your galley. They keep lettuce crisp, crackers crunchy, and cake and bread soft. For a large, frosted cake, you can make a cake saver by blowing up a large plastic bag and securing it with a rubber band. Toss salads in them too, to save washing a bowl!

A cloth bag can also save mess and dishwashing for you when you make cookie or cracker crumbs for a pie crust. I sewed a simple envelope from light canvas, and put a zipper in the top. Crackers can be pummeled in the bag, then poured into the pie pan. The bag must be sturdy, though. Plastic won't do.

A shaker—any container with a good, tight lid—can save washing egg beaters or mixing spoons. Use one to scramble eggs with milk, make instant pudding, blend nonfat dry milk, mix pancake batter. A small shaker, filled with one part vinegar, one part water, and three parts salad oil, blends a quick salad dressing base for your favorite herbs or spices.

Paper towels, too, are indispensable mess-moppers in your water-short galley. Use them for place mats, napkins, and cleaning cloths on sticky pans. Grate cabbage onto a paper towel for slaw; flour two squares of paper toweling as a pastry cloth for kneading and cutting biscuits.

This may sound like heresy, but I never grease a pan for a cake that will be served from the pan. A small flexible frosting spatula will remove the stickiest desserts without leaving a crumb. For a pan that must be greased, use a swatch of paper toweling to spread the shortening.

Scrimp and scheme all you will, though, the time comes when dirty dishes have to be dealt with. Try a 12-inch square of nylon netting for your dishcloth. It is the best thing I've found for whisking food off dishes, and it shakes dry in seconds so you never have to worry about souring.

In camp, or on the beach, make cleanup a family chore. While you eat, have two pails of water heating over the campfire, then put liquid detergent in one. Make an assembly line from soapy water to rinse to dish towel, and let each person do up his own.

Dishwasher detergents are too harsh for doing dishes by hand, but carry along a box of it (or bring a small jar of it from home) for those plastic containers that smell stale after a few weeks of normal washing. A soaking with this strong detergent and very hot water will work wonders, especially with the plastic bottles you use for mixing nonfat dry milk.

Coffee stains on your plastic camp dishes and cups? Chlorine and other harsh cleaners remove stains but leave the plastic porous so it stains more and more quickly. Use baking soda as a cleanser; wash cups immediately after using.

BAKING WITHOUT AN OVEN

All of our baking is done atop a Primus (pressure kerosene) stove using a cake tin placed in a heavy aluminum 11-inch skillet with a thick aluminum domed lid, and every recipe in this book that calls for baking can be made in such a skillet or in a Dutch oven.

For 350-degree baking, place a rack in the bottom of skillet or Dutch oven (I use the rack that came with our pressure cooker) and preheat, covered, over high flame for at least ten minutes. Then set cake tin on rack, reduce flame to medium during baking, and do not remove lid except to check for doneness late in the baking time. For higher heats, use full flame after thorough preheating. For lower baking temperatures, reduce flame or use an asbestos shield.

Although we have no oven thermometer, guesswork has never failed. We use it for cakes, pies, breads, coffee cakes, meatloaf, roasts, and biscuits. Even though baking temperatures are given in degrees in these recipes, you will come close enough by using the general instructions above. Your problem will be to keep the oven hot enough, rather than getting it too hot, especially on gusty days.

This same flexibility in rules can be remembered when you choose your baking pans too. We haven't room to carry a full selection of fancy molds, spring form pans, and cake pans in many sizes. Most of my cakes are made in an 8-inch square pan. I also carry one pie pan and one loaf pan, although breads and meatloaf will bake nicely in clean tin cans. In fact, the bread slides out extra easily because you can remove the other end of the can after baking.

If you are traveling light, there is no need to pack a special folding oven. We find them tippy and drafty, and they raise the temperature of your galley in hot weather. A heavy Dutch oven will hold heat better and distribute it more evenly. And ours also serves as a griddle and skillet. Although iron skillets can be bought with heavy lids, we prefer aluminum because it "seasons" as well as iron and yet distributes heat far better. Baking efforts in an iron Dutch oven resulted in black-bottomed biscuits, even though the baking pan had been placed on a rack in the pan.

For these same reasons, our only saucepan is a very thick, heavy one with a tight-fitting lid. Thin pans, made especially for camping, cool very quickly after being removed from the fire and are too thin for slow simmering or baking of thick dishes. Canned vegetables are, of course, heated right in their opened tins, over the camp stove or in a hot part of the campfire.

WHEN THE ICE IS GONE

More products than ever before are in the keep-for-ever class, thanks to modern canning and freeze drying. For vacations, you may want to try the delicious new freeze-dried steaks and chops, although we find them too expensive for full-time sailboat living.

At the other extreme of the sporting scale, there are still those sailors and campers who catch and smoke their own fish, and shoot, skin, and dry their own meats. The Galapagos is one popular stop for cruising yachtsmen who gun for goats there, dry the meat, and replenish their lockers.

As a compromise between living off the land completely, or relying entirely on expensive, commercial products, we can our own meats. It is cheap, surprisingly easy, completely safe when you use a pressure cooker, and it gives you a range of variety beyond such tinned stand-bys as corned beef, tuna, and salmon and dried products such as chipped beef, salt fish, or sausages.

Follow your own pressure-cooker directions for canning fresh meats. (If there are none, write to the manufacturer for instructions and for a special 10-pound pressure valve.) Basically, it's a matter of stuffing raw meat into a clean canning jar, and cooking under pressure for 75 minutes. With the two-part canning lids, any failures are spotted immediately. The rest stay safe and sealed for months. And, with only a little care taken in packing, breakage is not a problem.

We find that a pint jar of canned, boneless veal, chicken, beef squares, turkey, pork chunks, or ground beef is right for two. For a larger family, do your canning in quart jars.

With your own canned meats, menu variety is almost endless. Use beef chunks to make stew, soups, stroganoff; open a jar of veal for paprikas; make up the chicken with dumplings, the turkey to tetrazzini, the pork into chop suey, the ground beef in spaghetti and chili. The jars, of course, are reusable and the canning lids cost less than a penny each.

STORING
EGGS AND MILK

There are dozens of ways to keep eggs for long periods, and each voyager swears by his own method. The one common instruction is to start with eggs that have never been refrigerated.

Our grandparents packed fresh farm eggs in salt, where they kept for a year, or dipped them in water-glass, which can be purchased at pharmacies. Some people grease eggs with shortening, vaseline, or salad oil. Others dip them for exactly two seconds in boiling water. Anything that seals the shell will prolong freshness.

Milk is available in so many different forms today, it is just a matter of choosing the flavor you like best. One nonfat, dry milk brand, formulated especially for drinking, tastes best to us. To insure the smoothest taste, without the chalkiness of fresh-mixed milk, combine with water two to three hours before drinking and store in a cool place.

Liquid whole milk that needs no refrigeration, and a rich powdered whole milk are sold throughout the West Indies. So are tinned butter and margarine, although regular margarine will keep fresh without refrigeration for several weeks in a sealed container.

Cindy Brown of Fort Lauderdale makes reconstituted dry milk tastier by adding a sprinkle of sugar and a drop of vanilla per quart. Gloria Rollins, aboard *Gloria Luce*, told me that she uses coconut milk for puddings and scalloped potatoes. Dr. and Mrs. Doug Caldwell of Toronto add a few teaspoons of powdered coffee creamer to nonfat dry milk when cruising with their children. A few tablespoons of chocolate-milk mix will disguise nonfat dry milk too.

Cooling without Refrigeration

Porous pottery jugs sold in various parts of the world keep water cool. Jutta and Graeme Townes picked one up in Brazil, and the water from it really was cooler than air temperature because of tiny amounts of water that seeped through the jug and evaporated away.

The same principle is used in the Australian Outback, where cooling boxes are made by hanging water-soaked rags over a framework and letting the air blow through. This will keep things cooler in dry climates, but doesn't work quite as well in the damp air at sea.

The Doug Caldwells, who spent a year cruising the Bahamas with their children, carried lengths of surgical sock, the tubular material a doctor uses under a cast for a broken arm or leg. The fabric is pulled over a bottle and saturated with water; the evaporation of the water cools the contents of the bottle. (If the bottle is set in a pan of water, the sock will soak it up much like a wick.) To quick-chill a bottle of wine, the Caldwells saturate the sock with alcohol!

Does It *Have* to Be Cold?

Because we have roomy refrigerators at home, we get in the habit of chilling many items that can be kept safely without refrigeration. Cheeses and sausages traveled the world long before the days of refrigerators or ice lockers. Mustard, pickles, and relish will keep for a long time before they spoil. So will pancake syrups, jams and jellies, peanut butter, butter, and margarine. Many persons carry opened jars of salad dressing.

Of course you keep fresh meats chilled for safety, but we have kept cooked meats for second and even third appearances on our table. Packaged bacon doesn't last more than three days in warm temperatures, but well-salted pork and slab bacon, as well as cured hams, date back hundreds of years before the discovery of electricity.

Live by the safety rule of "when in doubt, throw it out," especially with fish, or salads made with egg and mayonnaise. But on the other hand, it really isn't necessary to go without many of the items you keep refrigerated at home.

LAUNDRY
AND LINENS

Elva Hefty, aboard *Leilani*, carries a child's small inflatable swimming pool and uses it dockside as a roomy, sensible basin for doing hand laundry. Cynthia Brown, whose husband Luke is a yacht salesman in Fort Lauderdale, carries a tightly lidded diaper pail for cruising and lets laundry slosh itself clean as the boat pitches and rolls. John Steinbeck, in *Travels with Charley* told how he let the motion of his camper wash his clothes as they soaked in a lidded plastic garbage pail.

Busy as you are, and short on water, the laundry still piles up. In cramped quarters and in mildew-inviting weather, it can't lie forgotten long. How can you cut down on the amount of your laundry and the length of your scrubbing time?

Some sailors tie their laundry behind the boat in strong nylon mesh bags, to plunge and splash through the water. Pete and Liz Elsaesser of St. Louis had twins in diapers the year they sailed their *Avenir* from Nassau to Nantucket. Liz dragged their diapers behind in a bag and rinsed them in fresh water to which she added laundry softener. She says they were the sweetest, freshest diapers she ever took off a line. One warning, though. Sharks will strike at almost anything, including your wardrobe!

If you wash by hand, you'll still find old-fashioned scrub boards in hardware stores and mail-order catalogues. Or, an easy-to-stow toilet plunger can be used to help work the dirt out of your clothes. Give all your laundry at least a ten-minute soak, to shorten scrub time.

Even if you find coin laundries as you travel, sorting and preparing the wash can be chaos in a cramped cabin or camper. We hang up two roomy bags in the head, one for white items and the other for colored. On laundry day, I can just grab the two bags, toss a couple of soap "pills" into each one, make up small bottles of bleach or other additives (to avoid carrying full-size bottles), and carry the bags to the coin laundry. It's then a quick job to dump laundry and soap into the machines, and I have saved money by bringing my own soap and bleach.

Bed linens become a special burden in hot weather and in water-short travels, especially when they must be washed by hand. Still, we find the disposable sheets far too expensive for our cruising budget. We carry extra pillow cases, to change them every two or three nights in steamy weather. It feels almost as good as a complete change of linen.

In Grandmother's time, beds were changed by removing the bottom sheet, changing the top sheet to the bottom, and then adding a clean top sheet. Don't forget to turn your mattress each time you change the bed, and use a mildew-chasing spray.

Clothes washed in salt water take eons to dry, and don't feel very clean when they do. Still, salt water can be used to stretch your fresh water supply. Scrubbing can be done in sea water and liquid soaps will suds nicely. Rinse in salt water, then once or twice in fresh water. A softener rinse helps.

When Norm and Mary Farr, aboard *Mary B.*, cruised Andros Island on short water rations, they did their laundry and bathing in salt water exclusively. Their comfort secret was to use lots of talcum powder, both on their bodies, and sprinkled on their sea-water-washed sheets. It helped banish the sticky feeling salt water leaves behind.

Most campers and boats have beds in irregular shapes and sizes, and many of them have to be remade each night because they serve as seats or sofas during the day. To cut down on bed-making time, sew the bottom side of each sheet in a contour shape to match the mattress. (Don't contour the top end if you want to use that top-sheet-to-bottom trick.) To save sorting time on laundry day, key linens by color for each bed.

You can avoid using any sheets at all by zipping up simple sleeping bags out of muslin or percale yardage, or out of sheets. These sleeping sacks are carried by traveling students at hostelries in Europe, and even by house guests who are only going to stay a night or two. They serve as sheets between mattress and blanket, or as a quickly laundered liner for sleeping bags.

Bare feet can grind extra dirt into bedclothes, but somehow it seems impossible to get children from bathhouse to bed without picking up a whole new set of dirty feet. Some mothers issue clean white socks to be worn in bed only.

SAFE SWAPS

Half the fun of wilderness living is to Make Do without running to the store. Here are some substitutes that have worked for us:

If you have no egg for baking, bake it anyway and increase baking powder measure by one teaspoon for each omitted egg. Cakes baked without eggs are usually more tender and crumb more easily.

A cup of butter in baking can be replaced by ⅔ cup chicken fat.

¼ teaspoon baking soda and ½ teaspoon cream of tartar will do the job of one teaspoon baking powder.

A satisfactory sour cream for cooking or baking can be made by souring tinned cream or evaporated milk with vinegar or lemon juice. Bob and Dana Sipeler, aboard *Merry Myrtle,* discovered this jury-rig sour cream and use it for beef stroganoff made from tinned salisbury steaks.

Brown sugar and white sugar can be swapped in recipes, cup for cup.

Honey or syrup can be used instead of sugar. Reduce liquid measurement in cake by ¼ cup for each cup of honey used.

3 tablespoons cocoa and ½ tablespoon shortening stand in for 1 ounce baking chocolate.

2 tablespoons water plus 1 tablespoon powdered egg equal one fresh egg.

HINTS AND HELPS

To store extra sheets, out-of-season clothing or little-used items safe from moisture on board or in damp campgrounds, place in a plastic bag and close flat. Then cover the closure with a strip of Teflon tape and seal with a hot iron. (The tape insulates the iron from the melting plastic as it makes the seal.) Don't let the iron touch the bag itself! And keep the strip of Teflon—it can be used again and again.

On long treks, where storage spaces must be filled with the most food possible, shun airy snacks like potato chips. Carry unpopped popcorn instead. Canned juices and fruit drinks are space stealers too. Instant powders make excellent drinks, and many of them are rich in Vitamin C.

To soften prunes for breakfast without cooking, cover with boiling water from your dinner fire and let stand overnight.

Aboard *Varuna*, they make cold tea by putting teabags and cold water together in a bottle and letting it stand in the hot sun for a few hours. Cool it in a shady place, a stream, or with ice.

Gloria Rollins, aboard *Gloria Luce*, discovered that delicious cold soups can be made without cooking by mixing dehydrated soups with water and letting stand in cool place or on ice for two or three days.

Buy fat wooden or padded hangers for clothes you will carry in your boat or camper closets. Thin hangers wear through clothes from the constant motion.

For hard-boiled-eggs-in-a-hurry, for use in sandwiches or casseroles, Cindy Brown of Fort Lauderdale scrambles the eggs instead of boiling them. When using powdered eggs, scramble extras at breakfasttime and use leftovers as you would hard-boiled eggs in luncheon and dinner dishes.

Soap and washcloths for all the family can be so much trouble! If you trek for showers to public facilities in campgrounds or marinas, you already know how many plastic soap dishes and washcloths can be lost in one season. And there is always the problem of drying washcloths before they sour. Solve two problems at once, by tearing off a sandwich-size plastic bag for each member of the family at shower time. Deep in one corner, squirt a tablespoon of liquid detergent or a blob of shampoo concentrate. In the shower, place a hand in the bag, soapy side out, and use it as a mitt to slather suds over hair and skin. Just a small amount of detergent makes plenty of lather, and it's the only soap you can use where shower water is brackish. After showering, simply throw the plastic bag away.

On your sewing machine, use material scraps to zip up drawstring ditty bags by the dozen in different sizes. You'll use them for cosmetic bags, carry-alls, shower supplies, a selection of first-aid materials. If your clothes are stored in hammocks, unjumble them by putting socks in one bag, underwear in others. Dish towels will stay clean in a hang-up bag; washcloths will carry in another, hand towels in another.

If you're an everything-in-its-place housekeeper, a selection of drawstring bags will help you sort belongings and keep them neat, even when stuffed into hammocks, duffel bags, or under-bunk lockers.

If you cannot buy butter or margarine in cans, buy fresh and remove from wrappers. Then press firmly into plastic containers and keep tightly lidded in the coolest possible place. If you travel without refrigeration, do not buy soft or diet margarines.

Keep one or two vacuum bottles handy and fill with boiling water from your breakfast and dinner fires. You'll always have hot water for coffee, bouillon, cocoa, or washing, without lighting a special fire.

Little folding net "umbrellas" are sold for keeping flies off food. Collapsed, they take very little space, and they are invaluable at campsite or dockside.

Of course we cut each other's hair! Even if you're not clever at barbering, ask for thinning shears at any store that carries a complete line of scissors. They do an excellent job of shaping hair, just by chopping through helter-skelter every two weeks. Trim around the bottom with regular scissors.

BREAKFAST

This is the most important meal of your day, especially on misty mornings at sea and in the early

chill of campgrounds. Scatter the children to find
kindling for the campfire or to sponge the heavy
dew from your decks. They'll come back hungry for
twice the breakfast they eat at home!

Pancakes

Haunt grocery stores until you find a mix that in-
cludes eggs and doesn't call for fresh eggs. We like a
pancake preparation that comes in envelopes,
sells for only 10 cents a packet, and makes a tall
stack of large flapjacks for two. Or, make them from
scratch.

1	egg	1 ¼	cups milk, any
1 ¼	cups flour		kind
2	tablespoons salad	1	teaspoon sugar
	oil or shortening	1 ½	teaspoons baking
½	teaspoon salt		powder

Beat egg with milk, then beat in dry ingredients until batter is smooth. Preheat griddle or heavy skillet until a drop of water dashed on it dances and dis-
appears. Grease lightly. Then spoon batter onto griddle for desired pancake size and bake until pancakes are puffed and bubbled with holes. Turn once
and bake until brown. This recipe serves four 4-inch
pancakes to four people.

Quicker than start-from-scratch pancakes, and
cheaper than mixes: multiply above recipe by five
or ten, mixing dry ingredients and cutting in
shortening with pastry blender. Store in covered
plastic container and use as needed, adding fresh
milk and egg.

To basic pancake batter you can add:
2 tablespoons imitation bacon bits or minced leftover ham

¼ cup chopped pecans
½ cup fresh or well-drained canned blueberries or pineapple
Thin banana slices (arrange on griddle and spoon batter on them)
One cup any instant breakfast cereal (fold in just before baking)
Dried apples (soak overnight, chop fine, and fold into batter)
Fresh apples or cut up pie-sliced apples from a tin.
One cup or less leftover cold rice (fold into batter)
Serve pancakes with butter and syrup or:
gravy made from bacon drippings
canned fruit pie fillings, thinned with hot water
jams, jellies, preserves, honey
hot applesauce
lingonberries or whole cranberry sauce, thinned with hot water
hot creamed chipped beef
your own syrup (make by stirring together 2 cups sugar, 1 cup water in saucepan until sugar is dissolved; add ½ teaspoon imitation maple flavoring, a drop of vanilla, and a drop of imitation butter flavoring)

Eggs Edith

This is a breakfast favorite with Jim and Edith Rohan, of Fort Lauderdale, Florida, from the days when they took charter parties down the Mississippi.

1 can pizza sauce   1-2 eggs per person
milk

Choose a skillet or saucepan large enough to hold the number of eggs you are cooking. Pour in pizza sauce and dilute with enough milk to make at least a half-inch of liquid in the pan. Bring to a boil, and poach eggs, spooning sauce over them, until done.

Shake-Up Scramble

No beater and bowl to wash, but you still can have airy, fluffy scrambled eggs. Put eggs, a few tablespoons of water or milk, salt and pepper, in a tightly covered jar or plastic container. Shake until frothy and pour into hot, buttered pan. Scramble until set.

Woodsman's Eggs

We cooked these crusty, bacon-bottomed eggs in an iron skillet over an open fire when we took Timmy, Jeff, and Chris Bott of Danville, Illinois, camping beside a stream in a private woods.

one-pound can bacon   1-2 eggs per person

Put entire can of bacon into cold skillet and cook over hot fire, stirring constantly, until bacon is separated and almost done. Remove from fire. Break eggs over bacon, cover pan, and return to fire for 3-4 minutes or until eggs are set. Separate into portions with sharp knife, and remove from pan with spatula.

Cheese Omelet

6 (or more) eggs   1 can cheddar cheese
1 tablespoon milk per   soup
  egg   salt, pepper
    2 tablespoons butter

Melt butter in heavy skillet with tightly fitting lid. Shake eggs, seasonings, and milk together in covered jar or plastic container until frothy. Pour into buttered pan and dot evenly with spoonsful of the cheese soup. Cover and cook over low heat until eggs are set. Stir and serve.

Eggs in Hash Nests

one-pound can corned beef hash	1-2 eggs per person
2 tablespoons butter	1 tablespoon cream
salt, pepper	(or evaporated milk) per egg

Melt butter in heavy skillet with tightly fitting lid. Spread with hash, cover and heat until warmed through. Make a hole in the hash for each egg with spoon or bottom of a glass, and break an egg into each "nest." Spoon cream over each egg and season to taste. Cover tightly and bake over low heat 15 minutes or until eggs are set.

Toast 'n' Eggs

Fry them together, and you won't have the usual last-minute scurry to keep eggs, toast, and coffee hot together on only two burners!

Cut a circle from each slice of bread with a biscuit cutter or sharp knife. Butter on both sides and place in hot skillet. Then break an egg into the center of each slice. Fry until bread is browned and egg has firmed. Then flip over and fry until bread is well toasted on the other side.

Break-Camp Breakfast

A quickie, but just as filling and delicious as the creamed eggs that took you hours. Always have hard-boiled eggs on hand for hurry-up dishes such as this one, and for rough days on the sea or trail when there isn't time to cook or make a sandwich.

1 can cream of
  mushroom soup
toast, biscuits, or
  crackers

4 hard-boiled eggs
¼ teaspoon curry
  powder, if desired

Warm undiluted soup in heavy saucepan over low fire until smooth. Quarter hard-boiled eggs, keeping one yolk in reserve, and stir into warmed soup. Add curry powder, heat thoroughly without boiling, and spoon over bread or crackers. Garnish with remaining egg yolk, crumbled.

Rice Cakes

An excellent disguise for cold rice left over from the night before. The idea was given to us by Mrs. Robert White of Urbana, Illinois, who makes these nourishing, golden "pancakes" for lunch.

1 cup cold, cooked
  rice

2-3 eggs
butter for frying
salt, pepper

Mix eggs with rice and seasonings to make a thin batter. Butter hot skillet or griddle and drop rice mixture by tablespoons. Cook until brown and crinkly, turn and brown other side. Serve with butter and syrup.

Hot Puffs

When you are near civilization and can buy refrigerated biscuits in a tube, simply cut them in half and deep-fry them. On the run, use biscuit mix to make these airy, crispy-shelled breakfast sweets.

10¢ package biscuit
  mix or 2 cups biscuit
  mix from a box

water or milk
sugar, cinnamon
oil for cooking

Heat at least two inches cooking oil in heavy saucepan over medium flame until hot (370-380 degrees). If you do not carry a cooking thermometer, test with a bit of dough. When it bubbles and begins to fry immediately, the oil is hot enough. Stir water or milk into biscuit mix with fork until dough is very thick. Drop the dough by teaspoonsful into hot oil. When browned, turn, and continue cooking until other side is brown and crusty. Drain on paper towel. While hot, shake gently in paper bag with cinnamon sugar or sifted confectioners' sugar until well coated. Serve hot and fresh with lots of coffee.

Canny Coffee Cake

Mix it up in mere morning minutes, and serve it hot from the oven. It bakes in less than half an hour, and it takes to many variations.

3 tablespoons butter	1 egg, if you have one
pecans to cover bottom of baking pan	⅓ cup brown sugar, firmly packed
10¢ package biscuit mix	milk or water

Preheat stove-top oven and use it to melt butter in bottom of 8-inch or 9-inch cake or pie pan. Remove pan while oven continues to heat, and sprinkle brown sugar and pecans evenly over melted butter. In bowl or plastic bag, blend biscuit mix with milk or water and egg, if desired, to make thick batter. For a sweeter coffee cake, add three tablespoons sugar. Smooth batter over brown sugar mixture in pan and bake 20-30 minutes in hot oven. Immediately turn out onto plate, and brown sugar glaze will melt down over sides of cake. Eat it hot.

For variety:

Mix with orange juice or prepared breakfast fruit drink instead of milk or water; sprinkle brown sugar-butter mixture with fresh grated orange rind or dried orange bits.

For each coffee cake, spread half a tin of fruit pie filling over sugar-butter mixture.

Try it with pie-sliced apples and a dash of cinnamon.

Soak dried apples overnight, sprinkle with cinnamon and increase brown sugar to ¾ cup.

Melt butter in pan, but do not add brown sugar. Make biscuit mix according to directions to make thick batter. Spread in pan over melted butter and top with streusel made by rubbing ½ cup brown sugar with 2 tablespoons flour, 2 teaspoons cinnamon, 2 tablespoons butter, and ½ cup chopped nuts, if desired. Serve directly from pan.

Spoon ½ cup marmalade or preserves into butter-brown sugar mixture.

Substitute raisins, cut-up candied fruit, or cut-up dried prunes for pecans.

Fruit Fritters

10¢ package biscuit mix	2 tablespoons sugar
egg, if desired	½ cup cut-up fruit
oil for deep frying	water or milk

Heat oil, at least two inches deep, in heavy saucepan over medium flame until a bit of dough bubbles and fries at once when put in. If using a juicy fresh fruit, like pineapple or berries, sprinkle with sugar and let stand at least 30 minutes, then drain. If using canned fruit, drain well. If using apples, bananas, or dried fruits, simply cut into bits to add directly to batter. Make a thick batter with biscuit mix, water or milk, sugar, and egg (optional). Stir in fruit and drop by teaspoons into hot oil. Fry on both sides until brown and crusty, turning once. Drain on paper towel. Serve hot with syrup, or shake in paper bag with sifted confectioners' sugar. Plan 2-3 servings from each package biscuit mix.

Cereals

For all their virtues of taste and convenience, we prefer not to carry cold breakfast cereals for camping and cruising. Even unopened packages stale quickly in damp outdoor air, and they are bulky and hard to store in cramped lockers. If your family cannot leave their favorite cereals behind, store them in plastic containers or bottles with tight-fitting lids, or wrap packages in plastic bags secured with rubber bands or ties.

You can pull more meals out of each pound of un-cooked cereals, and they prove much cheaper per serving too. Carry along quick-cooking oatmeal or the instant kind, cream of wheat, and a selection of other quick-cooking cereals. Try hot rice with milk and sugar too. Cook it in your pressure cooker.

Idiot-Proof Kuchen

On busy trips, who has time to watch yeast doughs to punch them down when "double in bulk" and then have the fire right before they fall? This rich, amazing kuchen gives you all the flaky, tender luxury of a real Danish, but it waits until you're ready to bake it—all night if necessary!

½ cup milk	1 teaspoon salt
2 cups flour	1 package yeast
1 tablespoon sugar	½ cup butter or
1-2 eggs	margarine

If using fresh milk, scald and then cool. No need to scald if you're using powdered or canned milk. Cut butter into flour and salt with pastry blender, then add eggs and slightly warmed milk into which you have stirred the yeast. Add sugar and mix well. Let stand in shady place, covered, about three hours and stir again. Put dough in buttered 8- or 9-inch pan and sprinkle with cinnamon-sugar, dried fruits, or nuts. Then cover and let it wait until breakfast time. Bake in preheated oven, about 325 degrees, until brown and flaky; 30-45 minutes.

Quickie-Sticky Buns

10¢ package biscuit mix, made according to directions or 1 tube refrigerator biscuits

¼ cup finely chopped pecans
¼ cup honey or maple syrup
3 tablespoons butter

Melt butter in heavy, roomy skillet with a tight-fitting lid. Add refrigerator biscuits, or prepared biscuit mix by tablespoons. Cover and cook over medium fire until lightly browned. (Watch for hot spots directly over flame, especially if your skillet is iron). Turn and fry on other side, about 12 minutes in all. Remove from heat and add honey or syrup and nuts, tossing lightly to coat biscuits evenly. Serve hot.

Trier Toast

It's the German way of making French toast, so I've named it for an ancient town on the French-German border that is a "must" stop for camping trips through Europe.

8 slices bread
2 eggs
½ teaspoon salt
dash nutmeg

jam
1 cup milk
½ teaspoon vanilla
sugar to glaze

Make four jam sandwiches with the 8 slices bread and soak briefly, coating both sides well, in a mixture of the eggs, milk, and other ingredients. Fry in butter until brown and crusty, then turn and sprinkle hot side with sugar as the other side browns. Flip over onto serving place and sprinkle other side with sugar while it is hot.

Fried Toast

Homemade bread doesn't toast as satisfactorily for us as store bread, maybe because it's hard to make thin, even slices. If you have no toaster, or want a crispy, buttery, new kind of toast, butter bread on both sides and fry in a heavy skillet until evenly browned. Try frying different bread too—banana bread, date and nut loaf from a can, Boston brown bread, fruit breads that you make yourself.

BREADS

Ships Bread

This recipe, which uses your pressure cooker as an oven, cooks over low heat on top of the stove. It was given to us in the Berry Islands by Bill Sparks, who has sailed his 24-foot cutter, *Roulette*, alone over thousands of miles in the Atlantic, Pacific, and Caribbean. The secret to its baking, and to its delicious crust, is a scattering of cornmeal. It is our seagoing staff of life.

1 ½   cups lukewarm water
      or 1 cup water and ½ cup sea water
1   tablespoon dry yeast
2   teaspoons salt (if using fresh water)
1   tablespoon sugar
4   cups flour
2   tablespoons cornmeal

Combine water, yeast, salt and sugar and let stand five minutes. Stir in flour. Let rise in a warm place about 90 minutes, or until double in bulk. Stir down, and let rise again. Grease pressure cooker thoroughly, then add the cornmeal and shake to coat evenly. Let dough rise once more in pressure cooker. Lock on lid, but do not use pressure regulator valve. Cook over low heat on top of camp stove for 45 minutes. Steam will escape through vent: do not remove lid during baking. Bread will be completely white and unbrowned on top. Turn out on plate. Sides and bottom will be a rich, crusty brown.

Singing Hinnies

We like these biscuits, drenched in tinned Australian butter, for breakfast. The recipe, and the next one, were given to us by Graeme and Jutta Townes, aboard *Hope* out of Sydney.

2   cups flour   2   rounded teaspoons
¼   cup cornmeal   baking powder
½   teaspoon salt   ¼   cup sugar
2   tablespoons lard   ¼   cup currants
              ½   cup milk

Mix dry ingredients. Cut in fat; add currants and milk to form a firm dough. Shape on floured board and cut into triangles. Brown on a hot griddle, two minutes on each side. Then reduce heat and bake five minutes more.

Rice Muffins

1 cup flour	½ cup milk
2 teaspoons baking powder	½ cup cold cooked rice
pinch salt	2 tablespoons oil

1 egg

Half fill greased muffin tins and bake 20 minutes at 400 degrees. For stove-top baking, put dough in 9-inch square pan and place on rack in preheated Dutch oven. Bake 20-30 minutes on high flame. Cut into squares.

Belaying Pin Bread

For beach bonfires or campfire cookouts, this simple bun can be served with butter and jam, or filled with hot dogs or sloppy joe.

2 cups biscuit mix   ⅔ cup milk

Add milk all at once to biscuit mix, stirring briefly with fork to form a soft dough. With floured hands, roll bits of dough about six inches long and the thickness of a fat pencil. Spiral around a peeled green stick, pinching ends to fasten. Bake, turning to brown evenly, over hot coals. Slip from stick.

Onion Biscuits

When you're close enough to city stores, make these tangy dinner biscuits with refrigerated rolls. On the trail, use dry biscuit mix. Most convenient: 10¢ envelopes of biscuit mix serve 3 or 4.

Melt ½ cup butter over medium heat in heavy skillet. Stir in 2 tablespoons dry onion soup mix and package of ten refrigerator biscuits which have been cut in half with kitchen scissors. Stir and turn until evenly browned. To use biscuit mix, simply drop prepared mix by spoonful into melted butter mixture. Turn until evenly done.

Stovetop Hoe Cake

1 ¼ cups flour	1 teaspoon salt
2 tablespoons sugar	6 slices bacon
	1 cup cornmeal
3 teaspoons baking powder	⅓ cup oil
	1 egg
1 ½ cups milk	

Fry bacon in heavy 9-inch skillet with tight lid. Remove bacon and crumble, leaving about 2 tablespoons fat in pan. Put all other ingredients into a plastic bag and squeeze until well blended. Put crumbled bacon in hot pan, pour batter over, and cover tightly. Cook over low heat until it tests done, about 15-20 minutes. Turn out on plate.

Double-Cornbread

3 eggs	10¢ envelope corn-bread mix or ½ package corn muffin mix
¼ cup milk	
one-pound can creamed corn	
2 tablespoons butter	thin slices process cheese
	½ teaspoon salt

Combine eggs, milk, corn, salt and mix in plastic bag and work to blend. Melt butter in heavy skillet; pour in batter. Cover and cook over medium heat about 15 minutes or until springy. Top with sliced cheese and cover again for a minute or two, to melt. Serve in wedges with more butter.

Steamboat Bread

2 cups flour (any combination of white flour, corn-meal, whole wheat flour, rye flour, graham flour, etc.)	½ teaspoon salt
	½ cup dried fruit (raisins, currants, cut-up prunes, etc.)
2 tablespoons honey or molasses	2 ½ teaspoons baking powder
	1 cup milk

Blend dry ingredients; add honey, milk, and fruit. Stir well and turn into a buttered mold that will fit loosely into your pressure cooker. A coffee can or other tin can will do, just so it isn't more than ⅔ full. Cover with lid or tie waxed paper over it with string. Place on rack in pressure cooker with about five cups water. Cover pressure cooker and boil, steam escaping, for 20 minutes. Then cook under 10 pounds pressure for 25 minutes more.

Scones

Classic baking powder biscuits bake beautifully on top of the stove. With butter and jam, they make a satisfying breakfast alone or with eggs and bacon. Or smother them with creamed chicken or creamed tuna, for dinner.

one 10¢ package biscuit mix
½ cup water, minus 2 tablespoons

Stir mix briefly with water and turn out onto a paper towel which has been dusted with flour or biscuit mix. Knead lightly until even consistency and pat into a round about ½ inch thick. Cut out with a small glass and place on hot, lightly-greased heavy skillet. Cover for about three minutes, then turn to brown other side. Remove from heat and leave in hot covered pan for five more minutes to cook through.

Banana Bread

In the Caribbean, most cruising boats carry a stalk of bananas, bought green, tied in the rigging. For camping trips, visit a wholesale produce market to buy these versatile fruits by the stalk. Hang them handy in your campsite to pluck as they ripen or, to hurry them to ripeness, store in a brown paper bag. Then, when you have a surplus of soft, brown-flecked fruit, you can use them dozens of ways in cooking.

⅓ cup butter or shortening	1 teaspoon baking powder
⅔ cups sugar	3-4 bananas
3 tablespoons sour milk	2 eggs
1 teaspoon salt	½ teaspoon baking soda
2 cups flour	

Mash soft, ripe bananas (about one cup) until smooth and continue mashing with fork to work in butter and sugar. Stir in eggs, milk, baking powder, and baking soda. Add salt and flour and blend well. Pour into buttered 9 x 5 x 3-inch loaf pan and bake in 350-degree preheated oven for one hour or until bread tests done. Turn out of pan and cool thoroughly before slicing, or wrap securely in foil or plastic wrap. Serve it cold with butter. For breakfast, butter both sides and fry until brown and crusty, or toast lightly on stove-top toaster.

Christmas Bread

No shortening to cream, so you mix this colorful bread with a fork! Sharon Heil, aboard *Gretchen*, who donated the recipe, says it is even better the second day.

2 cups flour	1 can whole
1 ½ teaspoons baking	cranberry sauce
powder	1 teaspoon grated
½ teaspoon baking	orange peel (or
soda	substitute from
½ cup chopped nuts	a jar)
1 egg	¾ cup orange juice
2 tablespoons	(or substitute
salad oil	powdered break-
¾ cup sugar	fast drink and
1 teaspoon salt	water)

Mix dry ingredients, then mash in cranberry sauce with a fork. Add remaining ingredients, stirring until just moistened. Grease a 9 x 5 x 3-inch loaf pan well, pour in batter, and bake 50 minutes, or until bread tests done, at 350 degrees. Remove from pan to cool, then wrap well in foil or plastic. Slice thin; serve with butter.

Same Day Sourdough

It's so outdoorsy, but such trouble to make the old three-day way. Now you can carry yeast in a package, and have satisfying sourdough in less than an hour!

⅔ cup lukewarm	1 cup biscuit
milk	mix
1 package dry	1 teaspoon vinegar
yeast	1 cup flour

Curdle milk with vinegar, then stir in flour and yeast to make a smooth batter. Cover and let stand 30 minutes in a warm place. Blend in biscuit mix and proceed as for biscuits.

SOUPS

Even summer nights can be cold at sea or in camp. A speedy, hearty soup can sometimes be the most satisfying one-dish answer for lunch and even dinner. The ingredients in these recipes can be kept on hand for weeks.

Alaskan Fish Chowder

This is a cold-weather favorite with Steven Ahlf who is usually elected cook on the salmon trawlers he crews aboard in Alaska.

3 pounds fish, any type	1 can diced clams (optional)
4 cans evaporated milk	½ pound butter
½ cup dried celery flakes	1 cup chopped bacon
4 tablespoons Worcestershire	3 large onions
3 tablespoons salt	1 teaspoon Tabasco sauce
4 cloves garlic	1 tablespoon pepper
	4 large potatoes

Dice potatoes and onions. Add bacon, celery flakes and garlic, and cover with water. Cook until potatoes are almost tender. Add milk, butter, remaining seasonings and, finally, the fish. Let it simmer 20 minutes.

Minute Minestrone

1 can minestrone soup	1 can bean-vegetable soup

1 can bean-bacon
   soup
1 small can sliced
   green beans
1 clove garlic
½ cup broken
   spaghetti

3 cans water
1 cup shredded
   cabbage
salt to taste
grated Parmesan
     or Romano cheese

Place all ingredients except spaghetti and cheese in a
large kettle. Bring to a boil, then add spaghetti and
simmer until tender, stirring occasionally. Serve with
sprinklings of grated cheese.

Clam Chowder

Mary and Jerry Staffney, whose yacht *Stayefree* we
met at Highborne Cay in the Exumas, always keep
these chowder ingredients on hand.

2 cans minced
   clams, with juice
3 large onions
1 can cream of
   celery soup
1 tablespoon thyme
4 tablespoons
   butter

2 cans or 3 large
   fresh potatoes
1 can cream of
   mushroom soup
4 tablespoons
   parsley flakes
2 cups reconsti-
   tuted dry milk

salt, pepper

Peel and cut potatoes and onions into bite-sized
pieces. Combine with clams and clam juice and
enough water to cover. Simmer until potatoes and onions are tender. Add both cans of soup, and a soup
can of water, then parsley and thyme. Simmer 30
minutes. Then add milk and butter, and salt and
pepper to taste. Simmer 15 minutes, cool for one to
two hours, and reheat just before serving.

Varuna *Fish Chowder*

Clint and Muriel Hinchman spend several months each year cruising the Bahamas. Muriel evolved this chowder after one she tasted at a famous restaurant.

two-inch square
  salt pork,
  finely diced
1 cup diced potato
3 tablespoons
  ketchup or
  tomato paste
  or tomato sauce
1 large can
  evaporated milk

2 or 3 fillets of
  any lean white
  fish (dolphin,
  grouper, sea
  bass, pickerel,
  etc.)
2 large onions,
  chopped
1 teaspoon
  curry powder

Sauté salt pork until slightly brown. Add onion, sauté until shiny but not browned. Add curry powder and stir until well wetted and mixed. Add potato, and just enough water to cover. Simmer, covered, until potato is tender, then add fish and simmer just until it flakes easily. Add tomato, then milk. Heat but do not boil; serve.

Swedish Pea Soup

Swedes religiously spoon up this soup every Thursday. Because the dried peas and salt pork can go anywhere with you, it can become a tradition with you too.

2 cups Swedish
  yellow peas
  (authentic ones
  can be bought at
  Scandinavian spe-
  cialty groceries)
8 cups water

1 pound lean
  side pork
2 cloves garlic,
  pressed into
  1 onion
½ teaspoon marjor-
  am or thyme

Rinse the peas, cover with water, and soak in large pot over night. If pork is extra salty, soak it separately in cold water overnight. In their water, bring peas to a boil and remove shells that float to the surface. Add pork and spices and simmer until tender—about two hours. Remove the pork and cut into fine cubes. Return to soup, salt to taste, and serve.

Mauffay

Hurricane Deliverance Day is observed about Thanksgiving time in the Virgin Islands with this soupy stew. Your shortcut is tinned barbecued pork that keeps in a locker until you catch a 2-pound fish.

2 pounds fish fillet, cut into one-inch strips	2 onions, chopped one-pound jar barbecued pork
½ teaspoon each salt, pepper, thyme	2 tablespoons butter

Sauté fish and onions in butter until onions are yellowed and translucent. Add a one-pound tin or jar of barbecue sauce with pork and cook slowly 15 minutes. Serve in bowls, over rice.

Peanut Soup

Well, it's different, and it is a classic southern favorite. Break it out far into your trip, when appetites are beginning to balk at "the same old things."

2 quarts chicken broth (canned)	3 tablespoons flour
½ cup butter	1 teaspoon salt
2 stalks celery, diced, or substitute dried celery flakes	1 onion, diced
	2 cups peanut butter (pint jar)
	dash celery salt
	1 tablespoon lemon juice

Melt butter and fry onion and celery for five minutes without browning. Add flour and mix, then gradually stir in chicken broth. Cook 30 minutes, strain and add peanut butter and the other remaining ingredients. Serve hot with a sprinkling of ground peanuts.

Fruit Soup

Serve this hot or cold, as a first course or as dessert. Dried fruit, light to carry and easy to keep, is a switch from canned fruits after your fresh food supply has become exhausted.

twelve-ounce package mixed dried fruit	¼ cup lemon juice
2 cups water	2 tablespoons cornstarch
2 twelve-ounce cans apricot nectar	2 tablespoons brandy, if desired

Cook fruit in 2 cups water for 20 minutes. Add nectar and a paste made from the lemon juice and cornstarch. Boil until thick. Remove from heat and add brandy.

Kött Soppa
(Swedish Beef Soup)

Gig and Chuck Grimm serve this soup-stew aboard *Yahoo* in Fort Lauderdale. Gig, who is Swedish, pronounces it like "shut soap-ah". Use fresh beef if you have it, or open a can of roast beef.

1 pound stewing beef, and a beef bone, or any meaty beef roast with bone, or short ribs	1 pound carrots chopped parsley
	4 medium potatoes
	1 medium head cabbage
	pepper

In a large, heavy pot, bring a tiny amount of water to a boil and pepper heavily. Add meat, and cook until tender and falling away from bone. Add water to cover, then carrots, cabbage, and potatoes, all cut into chunks. Cook, adding water to keep vegetables covered. When vegetables are tender, salt to taste. Serve in shallow bowls, sprinkled with chopped parsley. It's better the second day, and will keep overnight without refrigeration, so make enough for warm-ups.

Mexican Garbanzo Bean Soup

This recipe was sent by Mrs. Wilhelmine G. Goodman of Miami to her daughter, Mary Staffney, who lives aboard *Stayefree*. For fresh bacon, substitute salt pork, canned bacon, or imitation bacon bits.

3 strips bacon	small can
¼ cup chopped onions	chorizo sausage, sliced in rounds
¼ teaspoon celery seed	1 tablespoon dried bell pepper
medium can tomatoes or small can tomato sauce—or paste—in 2 cups water	1 can garbanzo beans, partially washed

Fry bacon, drain and crumble. In bacon grease, sauté sausage and onion. Add pepper, celery seed, tomatoes, and beans. Simmer together 15 minutes. Let stand an hour, then reheat before serving. Variation: instead of tomatoes, add 1 cup diced potatoes and 1 cup milk or water. Simmer until potatoes are tender.

Sunstantial Soup

Utterly wild! Dottie and Phil Sawin of Madison, Wisconsin, passed on this recipe aboard *Sea Lark*.

The Sawins, who have cruised boats all over the United States and traveled Europe in a camper, dote on it for lunch on busiest days when a pick-me-up is in order.

3 cans cream of chicken soup

¾ container sour cream or 1 container yoghurt (substitute ¾ cup reconstituted non-fat dry milk)

1 can applesauce marjoram, thyme, pepper and curry to taste

Mix together until smooth, adding the spices to taste. Serve as cold as possible, chilled if you have ice. Serves 4.

Portage Potage

Carry this pea soup in mere ounces and, when you eat it along a rushing Canadian stream, remember the French explorers who brought this fork-thick soup to North America.

1 package dehydrated pea soup stale bread garlic salt butter

small can sausages (cocktail wieners, Vienna sausages, etc.) or slices of hard sausage (bought unrefrigerated)

Make pea soup according to package directions. Butter bread slices (preferably French bread) on both sides, sprinkle with garlic salt, and fry on both sides until brown and crusty. Brown sausages well in skillet and stir into pea soup. Place a thick slice of browned bread in each soup dish and ladle the soup and sausages over it.

Bean Soup

A carry-along classic since clipper-ship days, and even today who can run a navy without it? There is no substitute for light-in-weight, inexpensive, nourishing navy beans, and they keep forever. Use your pressure cooker for fast cooking, or let them simmer in an iron pot all day over your campfire.

2 cups dried navy beans	½-1 pound salt pork or canned bacon
large onion, diced	salt to taste
1 can tomatoes (optional)	(depending on saltiness of meat)
pepper	water

Wash beans thoroughly, cover with water and let soak overnight. Dice bacon or salt pork and fry out in large kettle or pressure cooker. Add onion and fry until golden brown. Add beans and cover with water. Cook under full pressure for 40 minutes, and allow to return to normal. Add tomatoes and salt and pepper to taste, and heat to steaming. If a thinner soup is desired, add more water before second heating.

Quick Crab Soup

From Louise Villaret, this soup starts with half your work finished for you, because you use canned vegetable soup. Use leftover flaked fish or fresh, cooked crab if you can.

2 cans vegetable soup	2 cans water
1 can crab meat	1 can mixed vegetables

Simmer together 15 minutes and serve hot.

SALADS

Variety and texture contrast are the key words in salads that come out of your cupboard. Cruising in the Bahamas, we found supermarket vegetables expensive and wilted, with very little local produce available except in the few agricultural islands.

Camping and cruising, you can make use of the nuts, berries, and roots you find. For instance, we learned that green papaya, fried in butter, tastes remarkably like squash. Ripe papaya is a passable substitute for cantaloupe. Bananas, bought green in stalks, are seen tied in the rigging of most cruising sailboats. Sea-salted almonds wash ashore, and local mangoes in season are juicy, peach-like treats. Hearts of palm and sappodilla are also found in the tropic wilderness.

For long excursions, you can count on cabbage, carrots, onions, and potatoes to last a long time if they are kept in a cool, dry place. Oranges, apples, and grapefruit can endure the first weeks of your trip. Lemons, even after they have gone dry and hard, can be salvaged by soaking overnight in lukewarm water.

Still, long after the last lettuce is gone, your teeth are crying out for crunch. Nuts, added to almost any salad, give needed contrast. Finely chopped onions freshen a salad. Buy the milder ones for eating raw. Crisp croutons, made from leftover bread, add crunch to a salad made from canned vegetables.

These recipes have been chosen because their ingredients can travel with you for months.

Ambrosia

There are many variations of this southern Christmas favorite. Make it with canned or fresh fruit, with or without a splash of sauterne. This recipe was served by my mother, Mrs. Irving Hawkins of Gadsden, Alabama, when we camped for a weekend at Kentucky Lake State Park.

6 ripe bananas	1 cup grated coconut,
1 cup sugar	packaged, canned, or
6 oranges	fresh

Cut oranges in small, thin slices. Toss with thin-sliced bananas and sprinkle with sugar. Mix, then spread grated coconut on top. If using canned mandarin oranges and/or grapefruit sections, drain well before mixing.

Pickled Prunes

A new way to treat prunes. Put them in four half-pint jars, to pluck out of your locker and serve with a canned ham.

twelve-ounce package pitted prunes	3 cups cold water
1 tablespoon pickling spice	¾ cup brown sugar
	½ cup vinegar

Boil prunes, spice, and water for 15 minutes, then add brown sugar and vinegar. Mix well, cooking 5 more minutes. Pack into four 8-ounce jars and seal, or put in covered bowl. Let stand overnight before serving.

Sauerkraut Salad

It tastes surprisingly like cole slaw, except that this cabbage carries in a can!

1 size 2 ½ can
   sauerkraut
sprinkling dried
   bell pepper
¾ cup water
¾ cup salad oil

1 medium onion,
   sliced very thin
smallest size jar
   pimiento, diced
1 ¼ cup sugar
⅔ cup vinegar

Drain kraut thoroughly, squeezing to get out all juice. Mix with vegetables. Heat water, sugar, and vinegar until sugar dissolves. Add oil and pour over sauerkraut mixture. Sprinkle with pepper. Let stand several hours, or overnight, before serving.

Bean Quartet Salad

If you're out of celery and green pepper, forget them. There is still plenty of crunch in the canned green and wax beans, and in the onion rings.

1 can green beans
1 can green limas
1 cup sliced celery
small jar pimiento
   strips
1 ½ cups sugar

1 can wax beans
1 can kidney beans
1 diced green pepper
2 onions, sliced
½ cup salad oil
salt, pepper

1 cup vinegar

Drain all beans well and toss with other vegetables in a large bowl. Heat oil, vinegar, sugar, and salt and pepper to taste, to boiling. Pour hot over bean mixture, and allow time to cool completely before serving. For best flavor blend, then allow to stand several hours or overnight. And of course all salads are best if you can chill them first. Traveling without refrigeration, we find this, at room temperature, a cool contrast to hot dishes.

Red Cabbage Salad

I carry mayonnaise in 8-ounce jars, so I don't have to

worry about leftovers. Use the entire one-cup jar in this salad.

one-pound can   3 cups shredded
   shredded beets   cabbage
dash nutmeg   eight-ounce jar
                              mayonnaise

Combine cabbage and beets and sprinkle lightly with sugar. Salt and pepper to taste as you toss with the one-cup jar of mayonnaise or salad dressing and a dash of nutmeg.

Calico Bean Salad

one-pound can cut   one-pound can baby
   green beans   carrots
twelve-ounce can corn   small onion, chopped

Drain all cans and add to a large bowl in which you have mixed this dressing:

½ cup brown sugar   ⅓ cup vinegar
1 tablespoon salt   2 teaspoons celery
dash pepper   seed

Toss until well mixed and let stand for several hours for flavors to blend.

Garbanzo Salad

1 can garbanzos   small onion,
¼ cup vinegar   chopped
four-ounce jar   1 tablespoon dried
   pimientos, diced   parsley
dash pepper   2 tablespoon salad oil

Drain and rinse garbanzos. Combine with other ingredients and stir gently.

Coconut-Carrot Salad

1	cup flaked coconut	1 ½	cups shredded
¼	cup raisins		carrots
1	cup mandarin	2	tablespoons
	oranges, drained		lemon juice

salt to taste

Toss with ⅓ cup vinegar and oil dressing, mayonnaise, or bottled cole slaw dressing.

Wanda's Overnight Slaw

This crisp, flavorful slaw is an old family recipe from Mrs. John Cassil of Urbana, Illinois. When we camped autumn weekends at Brown County State Park in Indiana, she was elected to bring her salad.

1 large head cabbage   1 onion
¾ cup sugar

Shred cabbage in long shreds and layer with onion rings in large bowl or crock. Cover with sugar.

1 cup vinegar   1 teaspoon mustard
1 cup salad oil

Bring vinegar and mustard to a boil, add oil and pour over cabbage. Let stand overnight, in a refrigerator if you have one. Stir gently before serving.

Applesauce

Served hot or cold, plain or fancied, applesauce from cans is a tasty, tangy salad choice. Dish up this one with potato pancakes (from a mix) and hot tinned sausages.

1 can applesauce   ¼ cup white raisins
¼ cup brown sugar

Heat together until bubbly.

Hot Coleslaw

3 cups coarsely shredded cabbage	4 tablespoons bacon fat or salad oil
2 tablespoons imitation bacon bits	3 tablespoons vinegar salt and pepper to taste

Toss together in pan or skillet over medium heat until heated through and cabbage is glossy with an even coating of oil and vinegar.

P-P-P-Psalad

Peas for green freshness and vitamins, peanuts for crunch, pickles for tart crispness! Find English freeze-dried peas to keep in your lockers, or use tiny peas from a can.

1 package freeze-dried peas or 1-pound can peas, drained	1 cup salted peanuts ½ cup coarsely chopped dill pickle

½ cup bottled French dressing

Toss all together in bowl or plastic bag and let stand an hour, if possible, to let flavors blend. Spoon into paper cups.

Your Own Salad Seasoning

Walter and Jane Myers of Urbana, Illinois, have camped all over Mexico, Canada, and the United States. For a two-month tour of Alaska, Jane made up a big shaker of this seasoning mix to avoid a daily hunt for a dozen spice bottles. Vary it to suit your family's taste and sprinkle it on salads over a simple vinegar and oil dressing.

2 ½ teaspoons salt
1 teaspoon MSG,
   if desired
1 teaspoon garlic
   powder
¼ cup sesame seeds
1 teaspoon onion
   salt
1 tablespoon sugar,
   if desired

1 teaspoon dry
   mustard
2 teaspoons oregano
   leaves
1 teaspoon pepper
¼ cup grated
   parmesan cheese
⅓ cup poppy seeds

dried bell peppers and dried onion flakes (optional)

Mix all together in shaker jar with large holes and a tightly-fitting lid. Use to season greens or such cold canned vegetables as bean sprouts, green beans, or waxed beans. Toss with vinegar and oil to taste.

Your Own Mayonnaise

Shake it together in a glass jar, or blend it with a beater. Makes a pint of creamy salad dressing for your potato salad—and without eggs!

1 tablespoon sugar
½ teaspoon salt
½ teaspoon dry
   mustard
2 ½ tablespoons
   vinegar

½ teaspoon paprika
dash pepper
½ cup evaporated
   milk, undiluted
1 ¼ to 1 ½ cups
   salad oil

Mix all dry ingredients well with the milk, then beat in or shake in vinegar. Add 1 ¼ cups salad oil and shake or beat well, then let stand for a few minutes. If mixture is not thick enough, add the other quarter cup salad oil and shake again.

Cooked Salad Dressing

This is an excellent mayonnaise substitute to serve with greens, over hot or cold vegetables, with eggs for luncheon or to make a quick salad with canned potatoes.

2 tablespoons instant-blending flour	1 egg
1 teaspoon salt	¾ cup milk
1 teaspoon dry mustard	¼ cup vinegar
	2 tablespoons butter
2 tablespoons sugar	

In a heavy pan over very low heat, combine dry ingredients and stir in egg and milk. Very gradually add vinegar, then butter, stirring constantly until smooth and thick. For extra tang, make a package of instant sour cream mix according to directions, and blend in after taking pan from heat.

SALADS FROM YOUR SHELF

Shop for variety in all aisles of your supermarket for items you can serve as a salad course. Tuck away tiny jars of pimiento for color, water chestnuts for crunch, pickles and olives for the tart touch, pickled artichoke hearts for a luxury fling, chutneys in all flavors for a change, corn relish, pickled onions, nuts! The day comes when you crave them all as a switch from bland canned foods.

Toss whole Blue Lake green beans with vinegar and oil dressing, sprinkle with nuts, bread crumbs, or grated cheese.

Arrange tinned baby sliced tomatoes, drained, in salad dishes, and sprinkle with parsley flakes or freeze-dried chives.

Make toothpick-a-bobs with olives, pickle chunks, squares of cheese, croutons, pickled onions.

Serve up canned tomatoes with a sprinkling of sugar, salt, pepper, croutons, and grated cheese.

Add sliced fresh onion to pickled beets from a jar.

Serve sweet and sour cabbage from a jar with imitation bacon bits.

Sauce canned asparagus with vinegar and oil dressing and garnish with sliced hard boiled eggs and pimiento strips.

Mash whole cranberry sauce and mix with canned mandarin oranges.

If you have no celery to add texture contrast to potato or macaroni salads, try nuts, apple chunks or sliced water chestnuts.

Mix corn relish with drained, canned whole kernel corn to serve cool as a salad.

Cut canned whole baby carrots into strips, toss with vinegar and oil, and sprinkle with dried parsley leaves.

Soak dried apples overnight, cut into strips, and mix with sweet and sour red cabbage from a jar.

Make a fruit salad from any one can of drained fruit by adding cut-up pitted prunes, raisins, nuts, coconut from a can.

Slice tomato aspic from a can, garnish with freeze-dried chives.

Top rings of long-lasting Bermuda onion with canned mandarin oranges or grapefruit sections.

Drain pear halves and fill centers with salted peanuts.

Toss drained canned peas with vinegar and oil dressing and seasonings to taste, then garnish with quartered hard-boiled egg.

Stock jars of colorful apple rings and pickled pears to serve as salads.

Buy banana flakes to toss with canned fruits.

For fruit cup with extra pizzazz, soak raisins a few hours in wine or brandy, then drain and add to fruit.

Long-distance sailors grow their own fresh "greens" by soaking dried beans or kernels of wheat until they sprout well. Mix the sprouts with canned, drained sliced green beans and toss with vinegar and oil.

Marshmallows last forever in a tightly-sealed plastic bag if they are not allowed to become moist. Cut them into chunks with scissors; add to fruit salad from a jar.

VEGETABLES

These recipes were chosen especially to utilize only canned vegetables, or those with long-term keeping qualities. Count on cabbage to last from three to four weeks if you peel off leaves from the outside, rather than slicing through the entire head. Outer leaves will continue to protect inner portions and prevent the head from drying out. Potatoes and onions are traditional staples. Carrots will keep for a time. So will parsnips, turnips, yams, and rutabagas.

Shop throughout your travels for treasure finds in freeze-dried or dehydrated vegetables. The supply varies all over the world. Snap up freeze-dried mushrooms and chives, instant sweet potatoes, mixed vegetables, and packaged peas when you find them.

Store shelves change quickly, and vary according

to the parts of each country you travel. The store that carried canned artichoke hearts may not offer tinned celery. Another market may offer cans of black mushrooms or interesting vegetables you have not seen in tins before. Shop and keep shopping to vary your gad-about menu!

Carrots in Seedy Sauce

1 pound carrots, peeled and cut in slices	½ teaspoon salt
	4 tablespoons butter
	1 teaspoon celery seed
½ cup water	

2 tablespoons instant-blending flour

Cook carrots until tender and remove to serving dish, reserving cooking water. Brown butter in saucepan, then stir in flour, celery seed and salt. Thin with water from carrots and cook until smooth and thickened. Pour over carrots and serve. Makes 4-6 portions.

Grilled Bananas

There are said to be more than thirty varieties of banana in the tropics and they are served in any course from soup to dessert. Serve these steamy, fragrant fruits as a vegetable with pork, ham, or chicken from your grill.

one ripe but not over-ripe banana per person   honey

Cut a slit in the side of each banana with a sharp knife and pry away skin just enough to allow you to drizzle in a few teaspoons of honey. Let the peel close again and put directly on charcoal grill over hot coals. Cook, turning to prevent burning, until peel turns shiny black and banana is soft inside.

Creamy Cabbage #1

Shred 1 cup raw cabbage per person and place on a 10-inch square of foil. Bring up sides just enough to form a shallow cup and cover each portion with a tablespoon of fresh or tinned cream, or undiluted evaporated milk. Sprinkle with salt and pepper and a nugget of butter. Wrap very securely so that no steam can escape. Place on grill over white coals and bake, turning frequently, for 30 minutes.

Creamy Cabbage #2

Shred a medium-size cabbage coarsely and place in a heavy saucepan with ¼ cup water. Simmer softly until cabbage is tender. In a paper cup, blend 2 tablespoons instant-mixing flour with ½ cup milk. Stir into undrained cooked cabbage and toss over low heat until thick and creamy, thinning with milk if necessary. Add 1 tablespoon butter and salt and pepper to taste.

Creamy Cabbage #3

Shred a medium-size cabbage coarsely and place in heavy saucepan with ¼ cup water. Cover tightly and simmer until cabbage is tender. Or speed cooking by using pressure cooker according to directions. Remove from heat and do not drain. Add 1 can cheddar cheese soup and toss until well mixed. Salt, pepper, and butter to taste.

Grill-Glazed Carrots

1 pound carrots, peeled and cut into strips	¼ cup brown sugar, firmly packed
	salt, pepper
2 tablespoons butter	

Pile carrots on a generous square of double-thick, heavy duty aluminum foil. Add butter, salt, and pepper and sprinkle with brown sugar. Wrap securely, sealing to make sure no steam can escape. Cook over coals 40 to 60 minutes, turning often and keeping away from flames or hot spots.

Campfire Beans

one-pound can bacon	1 teaspoon prepared
small can tomatoes	mustard
or tomato sauce	2 cans baked beans,
2 tablespoons dried	1 ¼ pound each
green sweet pepper	large onion
3 tablespoons molasses	

Cut bacon into thirds and fry out fat in a roomy kettle. Add sliced onion during last few minutes of frying so that onion fries yellow. Drain off excess fat. Add remaining ingredients and simmer, uncovered, over coals or low flame until beans are brown and bubbling and onions are tender. Or let them cook for hours, covered, in a low, banked campfire while you hunt, hike, or fish. Hearty enough for a main dish. Or serve with grilled hot dogs or sausages. Plenty for six.

Beets à L'Orange

one-pound can beets,	salt, pepper
any style	1 tablespoon butter
1 can mandarin	1 tablespoon instant-
oranges	blending flour or
½ cup juice from	cornstarch
beets	

Drain beets, reserving ½ cup juice and place in saucepan with drained mandarin oranges. Mix flour and juice and heat gently with beets and oranges until thick and glossy. Add butter, salt, and pepper and serve immediately. Variation: substitute canned or fresh, cooked carrots for beets.

Sweet 'n' Sour Green Beans

one-pound can green beans, any style	3 tablespoons salad oil
2 tablespoons imitation bacon bits	2 tablespoons vinegar

Drain green beans and toss all ingredients together in pan or skillet over low heat until warmed through. Salt and pepper to taste.

Creamed Onions

12 small, whole onions, cooked or jar of cooked whole onions	1 tablespoon instant-blending flour
1 tablespoon butter	½ cup milk, cream, or evaporated milk
	salt, pepper

Cook or heat onions and drain. Mix flour into milk or cream and stir with onions, butter, and salt and pepper until thick and smooth. For added spice, try adding a dash of nutmeg.

Blue Lake Beans

2 cans whole green beans, drained	1 can French fried onion rings
1 can cream of mushroom soup	

Stir green beans and mushroom soup together in a suacepan gently until well mixed and steaming hot. Top with onion rings and heat a few minutes more until they are heated through.

Asparagus Soufflé

2 one-pound cans   1 can cheddar cheese
   asparagus   soup
     12 saltine crackers, crushed fine

Mix all ingredients in buttered ovenproof bowl and bake in moderate oven, 350 degrees for 30 minutes. Or mix and heat thoroughly over low flame in heavy, tightly-covered saucepan.

Sunstruck Cabbage

1 medium head cab-   1 teaspoon lemon
   bage, coarsely sliced   juice
1 egg, beaten   2 tablespoons butter
       salt and pepper

Cook cabbage until tender in covered saucepan or according to pressure cooker directions. Drain. Immediately stir in remaining ingredients, replace cover and let stand a few minutes until egg is set.

Whitecap Carrots (or Spinach)

about 2 cups cooked,   1 egg yolk (substitute 1
   hot carrots or   teaspoon corn-
   spinach   starch)
2 tablespoons butter   ½ teaspoon sugar
dash nutmeg   1 cup cream (substi-
                 tute evaporated
                 milk)

Combine butter, sugar, nutmeg, cream, and egg yolk or cornstarch and mix well. Add all at once to hot vegetable and stir over low heat until slightly thickened. Garnish with dried parsley flakes or crumbled cooked egg yolk.

Carrots Burgundy

We bought carrots in Nassau, so we could try the Villarets' recipe during our cruise through the Abaco Cays.

2 tablespoons butter	½ teaspoon salt
1 pound carrots	4 medium onions,
1 cup consommé (or	chopped coarsely
1 cup water and 1	1 tablespoon flour
bouillon cube)	

Fry onions in butter until soft. Then add sliced carrots, sprinkle with flour, and toss. Stir in consommé or bouillon and salt, cover, and simmer 15 minutes or until carrots are tender.

Vegetable Toss-Ups

For extra menu variety, combine two or more cans of different vegetables. To serve two, use small 8-ounce tins. For four, empty one small tin with one 1-pound can. For a family of five or six, you'll need two pound-size cans. Heat these combinations together, butter and season to taste.

Green beans or peas with small whole onions or mushrooms.

Combine canned sweet potatoes with a can of pie-sliced apples.

Mix canned shredded beets with a jar of sweet and sour red cabbage.

Heat canned tomatoes with crumbled crackers and serve with grated cheese from a jar.

Warm canned yams with a can of pineapple pie filling.

Quarter canned potatoes and mix into cream-style corn; sprinkle with imitation bacon bits.

Add a can of celery to green beens, carrots, or peas.

Stir together well-drained cans of kidney beans and green limas.

To a large (2½-size) can of green limas, add an undiluted can of pepper pot soup.

Bake acorn squash by placing cut-side down on a heavy skillet, lightly buttered. Cover tightly and bake over low flame until tender. Fill cavities with tinned peas or kitchen-sliced green beans, butter and season, and continue baking, cut side up, until vegetables are heated through.

For succotash, combine a can of whole-kernel corn with a can of baby limas.

Slice a tiny jar of pimiento into a can of dried cooked limas.

Heat a small jar of whole stuffed olives with whole-kernel corn.

Serve cans of stewed tomatoes hot and studded with whole ripe olives.

POTATOES, PASTA, RICE, AND NOODLES

Sailors and wilderness campers soon learn what orientals have long known: you can carry more portions of rice per cubic foot, per pound, and per dollar than of any other food. But put two cooks together, and you have a friendly argument over how rice should be cooked.

In Key West, Cuban-influenced cooks insist that rice should be cooked in large quantities of boiling water, then drained. Gourmets argue that it must be sautéed in butter first. The Chinese steam it. For burner-poor campers and boaters, here is the method that has worked best for us:

For each cup of regular rice, add two cups of water and one teaspoon salt in your pressure cooker. (Plan about one-fourth cup raw rice per person.) Bring cooker up to full pressure and remove from heat. Your burner is now freed for frying meats and warming vegetables while you wait for the pressure to return to normal, (Do not relieve pressure quickly by running cold water over pan.) When pressure is gone, your rice is tender, fluffy, and steamy hot! It's that simple.

Jutta Townes, aboard *Hope*, suggests an alternate method for a saucepan. Bring one part rice and two parts water, with salt to taste, to a boil in a heavy, tightly-lidded saucepan. Remove from heat and let stand, well insulated, for twenty minutes. (Jutta wedges her pan into a corner of a bunk and covers it with pillows.)

To Ritz Plain Boiled Rice:

Substitute canned stewed tomatoes for water; add 1 tablespoon instant onion.

Sauté slivered almonds in butter until brown; add to rice and water in pressure cooker before cooking, or stir in after cooking.

Add one tablespoon dried parsley flakes before cooking.

Toss one or two beef or chicken bouillon cubes into pan before cooking rice.

Substitute orange juice for water; add grated orange rind and a tin of celery or a sprinkling of dried celery flakes.

Drain a can of pineapple chunks and stretch juice with water to get required water measurement. Stir into rice, with pineapple, before cooking.

Instead of water, use coconut milk; sprinkle cooked rice with fresh grated coconut.

For each two cups of raw rice, add one package dehydrated chicken-rice or beef-rice soup mix.

Substitute canned beef bouillon or chicken broth, concentrated, for half the water.

Substitute tomato juice for water measurement; add instant onion and dried green bell peppers.

Stir one tin cheddar cheese soup, concentrated, into hot cooked rice. Garnish with chives.

Make soup-er flavored rice dishes by using one can of concentrated soup to one soup can water and one scant soup can rice. With bean soup, garnish cooked rice with bacon. With split pea, add a whiff of garlic. Try it with onion soup, vegetable, Scotch broth, pepper pot, even cream soups!

For a quick rice dessert, combine ¾ cup raw rice with 1 ½ cups water, ½ cup raisins and ½ cup sugar in pressure cooker or saucepan. Cook like other rice. Before serving, stir in ¼ teaspoon vanilla extract and a dash of nutmeg. Serve warm with tinned or fresh cream.

Peas and Rice

Made with tender, tasty pigeon peas, this is a main dish mainstay of the Bahamian diet. Buy pigeon peas in a can. Or substitute fresh or canned green peas, tiny red beans, or any small beans without sauce.

1 cup pigeon peas, cooked	salt, pepper, thyme
1 cup canned or fresh, peeled tomatoes	1 ½ cups rice large onion, chopped
2-3 slices bacon or salt pork	3-4 cups water

Cut bacon or pork into small pieces and fry with chopped onion until onion is soft and yellow. Add peas, rice, tomatoes, three cups water, and seasonings to taste. Bring to a boil, reduce heat, cover and cook until rice is tender, adding more water as needed. This makes four servings for a main dish and serves six as a side dish.

Indies Rice

Instant-ized for you with one of the new mixes. For a budget dish, substitute your own mixture of rice and vermicelli and add a beef bouillon cube.

eight-ounce package beef-flavored rice and vermicelli mix	½ cup shredded coconut
medium onion, sliced	½ teaspoon instant minced garlic

Prepare package mix according to directions and simmer with garlic and onion until rice is tender. Toss with shredded coconut just before serving.

Pilaf

Bake it long and slow for dry, fluffy rice. There are many versions of this dish from India. Serve it with warmed slabs of roast beef from a can, or with meat from your grill.

⅓ cup butter	1 cup raw rice
½ teaspoon instant minced garlic	2 ½ cups beef bouillon or canned onion soup stretched with water
¼ cup raisins or mushrooms or black olives	

For garnish: 2 tablespoons toasted slivered almonds or 1 tablespoon dried parsley

Sauté rice and garlic in butter in heavy skillet or saucepan with tightly-fitting lid. When rice turns orange, remove from heat and add bouillon or soup. Cover tightly and bake over slow fire, grill, or flame with asbestos shield for 50 minutes to an hour, checking after thirty minutes to add more water if needed. Before serving, stir in raisins and garnish with toasted almonds. Or stir in black olives or mushrooms and garnish with parsley flakes. Serves 4.

Rice Curry

1 cup raw rice	2 cups water
2 tablespoons butter	small onion, minced
salt, pepper	1 teaspoon curry powder

Sauté minced onion in butter in pressure cooker or heavy saucepan. Add rice and stir, then add water and bring to boil. Cook according to directions for cooking rice in pressure cooker or saucepan. Stir in salt, pepper, and curry powder. Serve hot.

Green Rice

Sharon and Bill Heil put aside their careers in nursing and engineering for a year to sail their sloop *Gretchen* in the Gulf of Mexico, the Florida Keys, and the western Bahamas. Sharon serves her Green Rice as a side dish, or as a main dish by adding a tin of shrimp, drained. Some recipes for Green Rice call for spinach. Substitute one small can of spinach, well drained and minced, for the parsley.

2 cups leftover rice (or cook ⅔ cups raw rice in 1 ⅓ cup water according to directions for cooking rice)	clove garlic, chopped
	salt to taste
	2 tablespoons olive or salad oil
	¼ cup parsley flakes

½ cup grated cheese   ⅛ teaspoon curry
    or 2 tablespoons   powder
    butter   small onion
1 cup milk   minced

1 egg, beaten

Oil heavy skillet or saucepan. Mix all other ingredients together well and spoon into pan. Cover tightly
and bake over low fire or flame with asbestos shield
for 30 minutes. Your pressure cooker, used without
pressure regular valve, makes an excellent "oven"
to bake this dish.

Hot German Potato Salad
(Lightning Class)

We served this at Highborne Cay in the Exumas for a
hurry-up cookout after a surprise haul of huge
crawfish.

2 one-pound cans   small onion,
    sliced potatoes,   chopped, or 1 table-
    rinsed   spoon instant onion
1 tablespoon freeze-   2 tablespoons mock
    dried chives   bacon bits
2 tablespoons vinegar   4 tablespoons salad oil

Toss together and heat gently until well warmed.
Serves 5-6.

Hot German Potato Salad

A Deutsch treat that is made without mayonnaise and
keeps without refrigeration. Make it early in the day
to let flavors blend. No worry here about spoilage!

6 medium potatoes,   ½ cup vinegar
    cooked and sliced   2 tablespoons in-
large onion,   stant-blending
    chopped   flour

1 tablespoon sugar	1 ½ teaspoons salt
dash pepper	¾ cup water
	6 slices bacon

Cut bacon in small pieces and fry with chopped onion until bacon is crisp and onion yellowed and soft. Blend water and flour together, and add with other ingredients except potatoes. Cook, stirring constantly, until mixture comes to a boil. Boil one minute and pour over hot potatoes. Cover until serving time. To reheat, warm over very low fire or low flame with asbestos shield. Serves 6.

Cheesed-Off Potatoes

Fancy you finding these delicious au gratin potatoes by opening three cans!

2 cans small whole	1 teaspoon prepared
potatoes, quartered	mustard
	1 can cheddar cheese soup

Mix all together and heat over low heat until well warmed. Garnish with parsley flakes or freeze-dried chives.

Potato Pancakes

Hot and quick from your griddle, they make a meal alone or with sizzling sausages. Serve them with applesauce.

2 cups grated	1 teaspoon instant
raw potatoes	minced onion
1 egg	¼ cup milk
	salt, pepper

Grate the potatoes into the milk. Then drain off milk and add flour to potatoes. Toss to coat, then stir in egg, salt, and pepper. Drop by tablespoons onto hot, greased griddle and fry until brown and crisp on both sides.

Instant Mashed Potatoes

Prepare according to package directions in a heavy saucepan with a tight-fitting lid, before you begin cooking the other dishes on your menu. Then set aside, under a pillow or over a cool part of campfire or grill, to "season" as you cook. This waiting time makes a world of difference in instant potatoes.

Dilled Potatoes

Scrub tiny new potatoes well and boil in small amount of salted water until tender. Toss with lots of butter and a sprinkling of dill seed. Very good with fish.

Lemon Potatoes

Scrub and quarter new potatoes and cook in small amount of water until fork tender. Salt and pepper to taste. Cut half a lemon in quarters, squeeze over potatoes, then add lemon pieces. Toss with lots of butter until well coated. Serve hot with fish and more fresh lemon slices.

Hurry-Up-Mom Fries

A specialty of Rita North of Youngstown, Ohio, when she and her husband took their two boys on a camping tour of Michigan. Cooking is made speedier because you grate the potatoes. No need to peel them either!

Scrub required number of potatoes well, and slice by drawing across coarsest cutter on grater or slaw cutter. Pile into a small amount of hot fat in well-seasoned skillet, salt and pepper to taste and cover. Cook ten minutes, turn, and cook ten minutes more, tightly covered.

Foil-Fried Potatoes

Slice scrubbed or peeled potatoes onto a large square of double thick, heavy duty aluminum foil. Salt and pepper to taste. Add a sprinkle of instant onion or fresh onion slices if desired. Drizzle with salad oil. Wrap very securely in envelope style so that no steam can escape. Bake slowly over grill or over low campfire coals, turning frequently, for 45-60 minutes.

Campfire Bakes

Some campers like to toss baking potatoes into the fire to let them char, then scoop out the tender white insides. We find it neater to use foil.

Wrap scrubbed baking potatoes tightly in foil, then pierce with large nail or skewer. Nest in white coals of campfire for 1 hour, or until wrapped potato feels soft when squeezed with gloved fingers. Or bake, turning occasionally, over well-started charcoal on grill. The nail halves your cooking time, so watch them! Peel away foil before serving, to avoid ashes on plates.

Colcannon

So easy, so Irish, and such a clever way to get vitamins into your family. Only one pot does it, for your potato and vegetable all in one!

small cabbage, shredded coarsely	five-and-a-half-oz. package instant mashed potatoes
small can boiled onions	salt, pepper, nutmeg

Cook cabbage in small amount of boiling water for five minutes. Drain, measuring water and adding to it to get water measurement asked for on potato package. Proceed according to package directions, mixing all ingredients right in with cabbage. Stir in drained onions, salt, pepper and a dash of nutmeg. Cover and let stand in warm place so flavors can blend at least 15 minutes before serving.

Power's Out Macaroni

No need to refrigerate this macaroni salad, because you don't use mayonnaise. Make it over your morning fire and let flavors blend all day. Serve it at "room" temperature, or slightly warmed.

eight-ounce package macaroni, any style
eight-ounce jar sweet pickles, chopped
small can peas, drained

1 cup cubed cheese, if desired
½ cup bottled French, Italian or oil and vinegar dressing

small sweet onion, chopped

Cook macaroni until tender. Drain and immediately toss with onion, pickles, salad dressing, and peas. Just before serving, stir in cheese cubes if desired. Six big servings.

Macaroni and Cheese

Many cheeses keep for weeks without refrigeration. Easiest for you, and foolproof for freshness, is cheddar cheese soup. Crushed cheese crackers make this family favorite doubly cheesy.

2 cups macaroni, any shape
crushed cheese crackers

1 tablespoon butter
1 can cheddar cheese soup
salt, pepper

Cook macaroni in a deep kettle of boiling water (about three quarts) that has been salted with one tablespoon salt. Or, use half sea water and half fresh. When tender, drain and stir in cheese soup at once, mixing until smooth and macaroni is well coated. Add butter, stir, and pile into serving dish. Sprinkle with cheese crackers and serve at once. Serves six.

NOTE: Macaroni and spaghetti double in bulk during cooking. For each one-cup serving, plan a half cup of pasta. Because so much of the cooking water is absorbed, never use more than half sea water for boiling.

Beefeater Macaroni

A budget main dish for meatless days, or a hearty starch accompaniment for grilled hot dogs or fried luncheon meat. Process American cheese will keep for several months unopened, but it goes fast in warm weather after opening. Buy it in small sizes that your family can finish in two days. This recipe takes almost the entire 8-ounce size package and leaves you a few slices for canapes or toasted sandwiches at lunch.

2 cups macaroni, any style	⅓ pound process-style American cheese
2 cups milk, any kind	
2 beef bouillon cubes	salt, pepper, paprika

2 tablespoons butter

Cook macaroni until tender and drain. Stir in milk and heat until steaming but not boiling, then add bouillon cubes and stir well. Remove from heat and fold in cheese which has been cut into half-inch cubes. Bake over low fire or flame with asbestos shield, for 20-30 minutes, or until mixture is thick and creamy. Season and sprinkle with paprika before serving.

Macaroni Redhot

2 cups macaroni, any style   ⅓ pound process-style American cheese cut in cubes
1 can tomatoes (about 2 ½ cups)
dash chili powder   2 tablespoons Worcestershire sauce
salt, pepper

Cook macaroni until tender, drain, and fold in remaining ingredients. Bake, tightly covered, over low fire or flame with asbestos shield for 30-45 minutes, or until liquid is absorbed.

Macaroni and Toothpicks
Great for texture contrast, and children love it!

1 cup macaroni   salt, pepper
1 cup milk, any kind   2 tablespoons instant blending flour
1 can, (1 ¾ ounces) potato sticks   1 tablespoon butter

Cook macaroni until tender and drain. In a paper cup, stir instant-blending flour into milk until smooth, then blend with macaroni over low heat until sauce is smooth and thickened. Add butter and season to taste. Immediately before serving, stir in potato sticks. Serves four.

Meatless Macaroni Meal
Sharon Heil, aboard *Gretchen,* dreamed up this quick-from-a-package meal, using tasty imitation bacon bits which really aren't bacon at all!

1 packaged macaroni and cheese dinner   2 tablespoons mayonnaise
1 can asparagus spears   2 tablespoons imitation bacon bits

Cook macaroni and cheese dinner according to package directions. Top with canned asparagus, well drained, dot with mayonnaise and sprinkle with bacon bits. Return, covered, to low fire or burner with asbestos shield, until heated through.

Noodles

Unlike macaroni products, noodles swell little in cooking. Boil them in large amounts of salted water, or a mixture of half sea water and half fresh. Plan about one ounce uncooked noodles per serving, more for big eaters or meals with few courses.

Toss 6-8 ounces noodles, cooked, drained and hot, with:

- 1 tablespoon butter, ½ cup slivered almonds and 2 teaspoons poppy seeds
- 1 cup fine bread crumbs which have been browned with 4 tablespoons butter
- 1 cup prepared instant sour cream (two packages), a dash of instant minced garlic, a splash of Tabasco, a little Worcestershire and salt and pepper to taste
- 4 tablespoons butter and 2 tablespoons dried parsley flakes

Scrambled Noodles

4 ounces noodles   4 eggs, beaten
            salt and pepper to taste

Boil noodles until tender in a heavy saucepan with tightly-fitting lid. Working quickly, drain noodles well and stir in 4 beaten eggs all at once. Cover tightly and set aside for a few minutes for eggs to "set." Salt and pepper to taste. Serve hot. A main dish for two to three people, or a side dish for five or six.

Rough Ride Noodles

The secret is in the shaking, shaking, and more shaking! Choose a pan with a tight-fitting lid. Better still, use your pressure cooker and then lock on the lid for the tossing.

8 ounces noodles
salt and pepper
to taste

3-ounce jar grated
Romano or Parmesan
cheese

4 tablespoons butter

Boil noodles, uncovered, until tender. Drain well. Quickly add butter and jar of cheese, clamp lid on pan, and shake vigorously back and forth and upside down, for several minutes. Season and serve immediately. Makes 8-10 portions.

MAIN DISHES

Our main dish menus rely exclusively on canned or freeze-dried meats, canned fish, fresh-caught seafood, and eggs. Our supply centers around the pint jars of chicken, turkey, pork, veal, beef, and ground beef which I can myself. For a larger family, put up meat in quart jars, or buy the two and three-pound tins of ham, corned beef, roast beef, and turkey which are on the market now.

Lobster Newburg

Bob Coristine, who sailed his *Hobo III* from Montreal to the Bahamas, served this when we met in the northern Exumas. His lobster, in 5 ½ -ounce tins, was brought from Canada.

1 cup white sauce from a mix

2 walnut-size chunks of cheese (substitute a can of cheese soup)

2 tablespoons Worcestershire sauce

2 tablespoons bottled lemon juice

five-and-a-half-ounce tin lobster

3 tablespoons ketchup

salt and pepper to taste

Stir cheese into white sauce until melted, then add remaining ingredients, ending with lobster. Heat through but do not boil. Serve on toast.

Burgoo for the Crew

Get out your biggest pot for this stew—it serves 15 hungry oarsmen. Ladle it steaming into shallow bowls, and serve with crusty rolls or biscuits.

1 quart canned boneless chicken, or meat from two whole canned chickens

1 pint canned beef cubes

2 cans small whole potatoes

1 can sliced carrots

1 pint canned veal cubes

3 quarts water (including juice from canned vegetables)

1 can whole onions

1 can celery

1 can lima beans

1 can whole kernel corn

ten-and-a-half-ounce can tomato puree

1 teaspoon pepper

1 teaspoon chili powder

2 tablespoons dried parsley flakes

1 can okra

1 (one-pound) can tomatoes

2 tablespoons salt

1 ½ teaspoons dry mustard

dash Tabasco

Simmer together an hour, to allow flavors to blend. Better still, stir it up early in the day, allow to cool, and reheat at dinner time.

Charcoal Grouper Lazarus

Dick and Bev Lazarus aboard *Down Easter* in the Virgin Islands cook this delicious fish on their stern-mounted charcoal grill.

1 grouper (or sea bass)	2 shakes garlic salt
juice of ½ lemon	1 tablespoon soy sauce
1 ½ ounces dry vermouth	¼ cup butter
½ cup water	

Warm marinade in a small pot over coals. Cook grouper slowly on grill, or in a hamburger press to make turning easier, turning and basting frequently with marinade. Serve with foil-wrapped baked potatoes, baked in coals.

Ham Casserole

Rollie and Carolyn Payne, aboard *Bessie Virginia*, smother canned ham in black cherry preserves. Ann Bolderson, on *Nymph Errant,* bakes ham with cherry pie filling. For a fruity one-dish ham dinner, use dried peaches:

12 ounces dried peaches, quartered	⅔ cup milk
one-pound canned ham, cubed	1 ¼ cups water
1 package scalloped potato mix	2 ten-ounce cans chicken broth
	2 tablespoons butter
	¼ cup raisins

Cook peaches in water fifteen minutes, or according to pressure cooker directions. Drain. Add cubed ham, dry potatoes and raisins. Sprinkle with seasoning mix from the potato package. Heat chicken broth and stir in; then add milk and butter. Simmer very carefully over low heat, tightly covered, for 30 minutes.

Chicken Curry

When we met Tony and Trudy Mather in Nassau, aboard the famous Expo-built schooner *Atlantica*, they were on their way to Grenada. Trudy spirited this curry out of a locker for a potluck dinner.

2 tablespoons butter	2 onions, thinly sliced
1 can carrots, drained	1 can mushrooms, drained
one-and-a-half-ounce box raisins	1 tablespoon curry powder, or more
1 can cooked whole chicken	salt and pepper

Drain chicken, reserving broth, and pick meat from bones. Melt butter and sauté onions until lightly browned. Add curry powder, carrots, mushrooms, raisins and chicken, and stir to brown lightly. Add chicken broth and simmer lightly until mixture is heated through. Salt and pepper to taste. Serve with grated coconut and mango chutney on a bed of rice.

Fish and Chips

Carolyn and Andy Van Herk were six-week newly-weds when we met their *Bluefin* at Stocking Island, Bahamas. Andy, who is from Halifax, likes his fish the Nova Scotia way.

Heat an inch of oil in a heavy skillet. Cut potatoes, one per person, into chunks like large French fries. While they are cooking in the oil, make a batter of:

¾ cup milk	¼ cup flour
⅛ teaspoon salt	1 egg

Wash and drain fillets of fish (the Van Herks like grouper best), cut in serving-size pieces, and salt and pepper them. Dip in the batter, and fry in heated oil until crisp and brown. Serve with the golden brown fried potatoes.

Crab Wilmington

Jackie Bird, aboard *Halcyon*, reaches for canned crab to make this creamy concoction. We like it served with toast.

1 large can crab-meat, flaked	1 teaspoon instant onion flakes
1 teaspoon dried parsley flakes	½ teaspoon Worcestershire
1 envelope white sauce mix	

Prepare white sauce according to package directions, and add other ingredients. Salt and pepper to taste and add more Worcestershire if desired. Heat thoroughly. Serve over toast, rice etc.

Snitz and Knepp

Use your pressure cooker and a canned ham to make this Pennsylvania Dutch invention.

one-and-a-half-pound canned ham, sliced	five-ounce package dried apples
2 tablespoons brown sugar	10¢ package biscuit mix
½ cup water	

Add water according to package directions, to cook apples until tender. If not using a pressure cooker, soak the apples overnight to speed cooking. Stir in brown sugar and add ham. When juice is bubbling, add by spoonful dumplings that you have made by adding ½ cup water to the package of biscuit mix.

Simmer ten minutes uncovered, then ten minutes more tightly covered.

Fried Rice

Jane Sloman, aboard *Murisue* out of Fort Lauderdale, told me about this quickie. We open a canned ham at breakfast time, fry a few slices with eggs, and save the leftovers for this dinner treat.

½ pound ham or any cooked meat, cut in small pieces	1 teaspoon Worcestershire
small onion, chopped	1 tablespoon fat (preferably bacon drippings)
1 cup instant rice	2 eggs (optional)

Fry onion lightly in fat, then add ham and rice to brown slightly. Add Worcestershire and one cup of water. Bring to boiling, cover, and remove from heat. Let steam 7 minutes and serve. Or, after steaming, return to heat, push fried rice aside and add a little butter. Then scramble 2 eggs in pan and mix with the rice before serving.

Corned Beef and Cabbage

Bill Sparks, aboard the 24-foot cutter *Roulette*, carries lots of corned beef. It is more than a versatile, nourishing, easily-stored meat. He finds it a universally-valued trading medium and has bartered it for fresh fish and other stores. Half an hour after reaching Bimini in a very rough Gulfstream crossing, we sat down to this Saint Patrick's Day favorite.

Medium cabbage, in chunks	Carrots as desired, sliced or halved
Potatoes as desired, in quarters	1 can corned beef
	1 cup water
1 beef bouillon cube	

Place all ingredients in pressure cooker and heat. Bring up to pressure and cook for eight minutes. Allow pressure to dissipate by removing cooker from heat. Serve hot. Each can of beef serves two.

Tongan Stew

Jutta and Graeme Townes sailed their 30-foot cutter, *Hope,* from Australia to America via Kenya, South Africa, Brazil, and the West Indies. This recipe was given to them by friends in Africa, whose Tongan crew members voted it a favorite.

2 large onions, sliced	1 can green beans
1 can tomatoes	salt, if needed
½ teaspoon pepper	(depending on
1 can corned beef	the saltiness of
	your beef)
	butter or
	cooking fat

Fry onions in a little butter or fat. Add the corned beef, vegetables, and spices and simmer until blended and well heated. Serve over rice.

Corned Beef Patties

This recipe and the following one are *Hope* originals. The hot, crusty crunch of these fried cakes is a welcome contrast in a diet of bland, canned meats.

1 can corned beef	Cooking fat
1 egg	1 cup cold
salt and pepper	mashed potato
to taste	1 onion, diced
bread crumbs	

Blend beef, potato, egg, onion and spices. Add bread crumbs as necessary to make a mixture thick enough to be formed into patties. Shape, then coat with more bread crumbs or flour. Fry in hot fat until well browned and crisp.

Corned Beef Stew

Tinned cream gives a whole new character to corned beef. Jutta Townes serves this over rice, potatoes, or noodles. We like it with canned potato sticks, for texture contrast.

> 1 can corned beef   1 can carrots
> four-ounce tin cream

Blend corned beef and cream and heat gently. Add carrots, mix and heat through.

Steamed Fish

Another way to use the thick, rich canned cream that is sold in most parts of the world. Aboard *Hope*, they fished for grouper and dolphin, to cook this way.

> Any large fish   2 large onions,
>   steak (dolphin,   sliced
>   grouper, sword-   2 tablespoons
>   fish, tuna) or   paprika
>   fish fillets,   salt as needed
>   rolled and   four-ounce tin cream
>   secured with   2 bay leaves
>   toothpicks   butter

Fry onions in butter until soft and yellow. On the bed of onions, arrange fillets, or fish steaks that are about 1½ inches thick. Mix paprika, cream, bay leaves, and salt and pour over fish. Cover tightly and cook over low flame for 35 minutes. For thinner steaks or fillets, reduce cooking time. The creamy sauce also tastes good on noodles.

Skillet Tagliarini

Rustle up this hearty Italian dish in one pot. It is best made with fresh ground beef, but it takes well to home-canned beef too. For speedier cooking, can ground beef with onion.

1	pound ground beef, browned or 1 pint home canned hamburger		salt and pepper to taste
1	teaspoon oregano	¾	cup chopped onion
2	tablespoons dried bell pepper	2	cans tomatoes
1	can whole-kernel corn	1	can pitted ripe olives
4	ounces noodles, uncooked	¼	cup grated Parmesan cheese or ¼ pound grated Cheddar

Mix together the beef, oregano, pepper, corn, onion, tomatoes, olives, and seasonings, including liquid from canned corn but not liquid from olives, in skillet and bring to a boil. Add noodles, cover and simmer over low flame for 25 minutes. Remove lid and cook gently for another ten minutes, stirring occasionally. Fold in cheese and serve.

Hobo Dinner

Save your coffee cans for this campfire meal. Everyone makes and cooks his own, which is half the fun. Children love the novelty of it as well as the chance to vary and eliminate ingredients to their own tastes. For four one-pound coffee cans:

1	pound ground chuck	large onion, sliced thin

2 large potatoes	1 can corn, peas
1 large can	or kitchen-sliced
tomatoes	green beans
2 carrots	salt and pepper

Put ground chuck patty in bottom of each coffee tin, then add layers of thin-sliced potato, half slices carrots, tomatoes, and canned vegetable. Cover. Cook 45 minutes or until potatoes and carrots are tender, on grill or in spots directly in campfire where heat is not too intense, moving frequently. Of course, you'll eat directly from the can. Or, arrange these same dinner makings on double-thick squares of heavy aluminum foil. Fold securely and cook over hot coals, turning often, for about 30 minutes.

Mountain Pork Chops

Russ and Maizie Hawkins, who camp in the Adirondack Mountains of New York State, recommend this skillet meal for the camp stove or a bed of coals.

4 thick, meaty pork	eight-ounce can
chops or 1 quart	tomato sauce
home-canned	2 tablespoons
pork cubes	dried bell pepper
2 one-pound cans	medium onion,
kidney beans,	chopped
drained	2 teaspoons
	chili powder

Sear fresh pork chops in hot skillet. Pour off any excess fat. Add remaining ingredients and simmer, tightly covered, for 45 minutes—less if using canned meat.

Reuben Pie

A bit of Broadway deli, baked over a campstove flame in your oven or skillet.

one-pound can
  corned beef hash
1 egg
1 teaspoon caraway
  seeds
1 cup flour
¾ teaspoon salt
¾ cup water
1 teaspoon
  baking powder

1 cup shredded
  Swiss cheese (buy
  an unrefrigerated
  Gruyère)
eight-ounce can
  sauerkraut,
  well drained
dash coarse
  pepper
⅔ cup shortening

Mix hash, cheese, sauerkraut, caraway, and pepper
in small bowl, and form into a mound. Set aside.
Combine flour, baking powder, salt, egg, shortening,
and water and beat very well. Pour batter into 9-inch
pie pan. Gently place mound of corned beef mixture
in center of batter. Place pie on rack in pre-heated
covered skillet. Bake 40 to 45 minutes over high heat,
or at 425 degrees. Serve in wedges.

Tropic Meal-in-a-Bowl
On hottest days, mix up this hearty main dish salad
early in the day, to eat cold at dinner time.

3 cups warm rice
¾ teaspoon salt
2 tablespoons
  dry mustard
1½ teaspoons sugar
1 cup diced cooked
  ham or other
  leftover meat
1 tablespoon
  freeze-dried chives
sprinkling dried
  parsley for
  garnish

2 tablespoons
  vinegar
¼ cup salad oil
2 tablespoons
  water
3 tablespoons
  chopped green
  pepper, celery,
  nuts, hearts of
  palm, or sliced
  water chestnuts
½ cup cooked
  green vegetable

Mix salt, mustard, 2 tablespoons water, and sugar into oil and stir into warm rice. Cool and add other ingredients, tasting to add more salt if needed. Sprinkle with parsley. Serve cold.

Chunking Chicken Salad

A too-hot-to-cook-day dinner, made crisp with the toothsome texture of canned bean sprouts. Use left-over chicken, or open a tin.

Meat from one canned whole chicken, diced	1 ½ cups celery, or 1 can celery, drained
1 can bean sprouts, well drained	2 tablespoons soy sauce
pepper to taste	eight-ounce jar
salt if needed	mayonnaise

Toss together and serve with canned potato sticks.

Mexidumpling Stew

2 cans chili	1 cup biscuit mix
3 tablespoons cornmeal	eight-ounce can cream-style corn

Heat canned chili to steaming. Blend biscuit mix, cornmeal, and corn. Drop by teaspoons on hot chili. Simmer very gently, uncovered, for ten minutes. Then cover and simmer ten minutes more.

Roamer's Ragout

A budget switch on beef with wine. Grape juice adds a new flavor to canned beef.

2 pounds stewing beef or 2-pound tin roast beef or 1 quart home-canned beef chunks	3 tablespoons vinegar
	medium onion, diced
	1 teaspoon oregano

1 cup unsweetened	bay leaf
grape juice	small can
2 tablespoons oil	tomato sauce

Put all ingredients in heavy covered skillet or pot and simmer until flavors are well blended. If using fresh meat, bring to boil and simmer 1½-2 hours, until the meat is tender. Serve with rice, noodles or potatoes.

Spam Slam

Your own imagination will find lots of ways to cook canned luncheon meat. One of the simplest ways is suggested by Mrs. Henry Groene of Valley City, Ohio, for hurry-up meals at home or on the road. Luncheon meats from both America and Denmark are safe, inexpensive, and available around the world. Be wary, though! Don't buy in case-size lots until you've sampled a new brand. There is a great variety in taste, texture, and quality.

1 can luncheon	3 medium potatoes,
meat, cubed	cubed
large onion,	1 tablespoon
diced	shortening

Fry potatoes in hot shortening for five minutes, then add onions and meat. Cover and cook for 15 minutes, stirring often. Add salt and pepper to taste.

Hunter's Cabin Stuffing

Take dried fruit and packaged croutons on a hunting trip. This Mexican stuffing is enough for a five-pound bird, or 6 one-pound game hens.

twelve-ounce package	½ teaspoon each
pitted prunes	salt and nutmeg,
1 cup sherry	dash pepper

2 cups unseasoned croutons	3 tablespoons butter
five-ounce package dried apples	small package blanched almonds

Cut up prunes and apple rings and add to boiling sherry. Remove from heat, cover, and let stand 10 minutes. Drain off sherry and add hot water to make 1 cup. Melt in butter, and combine with all other ingredients. Stuff and bake with your day's bag, or bake with a tinned ham that has been browned well on both sides and heated through.

Fruity Chicken

Stock your lockers with a full variety of canned soups to speed casseroles and to make sauces for vegetables.

4 large fresh chicken thighs or 4 large chicken thighs canned at home in a quart jar	1 can cream of chicken soup butter 4 canned peach halves, drained

Brown chicken lightly in a little butter, and pour off excess fat. If using canned chicken, add broth from jar and all other ingredients. Heat through and serve. With fresh chicken, add cream of chicken soup and ¼ cup water and simmer gently for 45 minutes. Add peaches, heat and serve.

Beef Fancy-Up

1 pint home-canned beef cubes or 1 pound fresh sirloin cubes	1 medium-size can small onions
1 can golden mushroom soup	1 package instant sour cream made according to directions
salt, pepper	

Heat all together gently, adding sour cream last, taking care not to let it come to a boil. Serve over wide buttered noodles that have been sprinkled with parsley flakes. Variation: substitute ¼ cup dry red wine for sour cream. Serve on noodles. When using fresh sirloin cubes, brown well and simmer until tender before adding wine or sour cream.

Stuffed Cabbage **Royal Star**

A man's main dish, made for us in the Bahamas by Wally Johnson, captain of the *Royal Star* out of Dover, New Hampshire. Make extra rice the night before and mask the leftovers in this pressure cooker version of a classic dish.

1 ½ cups cooked rice	8-10 large cabbage leaves
medium onion, chopped	1 can corned beef
dash pepper	1 egg (optional)

Mix rice, pepper, corned beef, onion, and egg. Wilt cabbage leaves by placing in pressure cooker (not under pressure) for a few minutes with rapidly boiling water. Remove leaves, leaving 1 cup water in cooker. Place equal portions of corned beef mixture in center of each cabbage leaf, fold over and roll. Place on rack in pressure cooker and cook 8 minutes under pressure. Cool at once under cold running water or, to keep warm longer, let pressure return to normal by setting aside, away from fire. Wally likes these stuffed cabbages served with soy sauce and has been known to eat leftovers cold for breakfast. Serves 4 generously.

Salmon Newburg

One-pound can salmon, drained, flaked, and boned
small jar mushrooms, drained
2 tablespoons butter
1½ tablespoons instant blending flour
1 cup milk
½ cup cream or evaporated milk
dash Worcestershire
1 teaspoon salt
dash cayenne
1 teaspoon lemon juice
3 tablespoons sherry (optional)

Stir flour with milk and cream in cold saucepan, then heat, stirring, over low heat until thickened. Add remaining ingredients, except for sherry and heat gently until well warmed through. Add sherry and serve over hot, buttered toast.

Steamed Salmon Loaf

An Alaskan recipe from pilot Bob Leonard, adaptable for nomad cooking because you can use canned salmon—and speed cooking by using your pressure cooker.

4 eggs, beaten, or equivalent in powdered eggs and water
4 soda crackers, crumbled
1 tablespoon instant onion
one-pound can salmon, drained
4 tablespoons melted butter
1 tablespoon celery flakes
dash pepper

Combine all ingredients in a plastic bag and knead to blend. Pour into buttered baking dish or large tin can and place on rack in pressure cooker with one cup water. Cook under pressure for 8 minutes. Cool at once. Remove can, rack, and water and then use pressure cooker to make sauce:

one-pound can peas	1 cup milk
¼ cup water or liquid from salmon	1 tablespoon cornstarch
1 tablespoon butter	1 tablespoon catsup
dash pepper	salt to taste

Stir cornstarch into milk and other liquid in pressure pan. Cook over low heat, stirring constantly, until smooth and thick. Stir in other ingredients and heat thoroughly without boiling. Spoon over sliced, hot salmon loaf.

Chicken Webfoot

For two days, Emmita and David Weiher were just voices out of the storm as we both battled through a norther in the open sea, 125 miles east of San Salvador. We kept in touch by setting up radio dates and recounting a growing list of casualties—their genoa halyard, our self-steering rudder, their dinghy, then our dinghy.

We ended up back at peaceful Hawk's Nest Creek on Cat Island where Emmita and I met, bemoaned the messes in our soggy cabins, and swapped recipes.

1 ½ cups grated cheddar cheese (substitute 1 can cheddar cheese soup and omit milk	1 can cream of mushroom soup
butter	1 teaspoon salt
½ cup milk	meat from one whole canned chicken
1 can chop suey vegetables, drained	2 cans French-sliced green beans, drained
	⅓ cup chopped onion
1 can French Fried onion rings	

In roomy saucepan or skillet, sauté onion in a little butter. Then add remaining ingredients except for cheese and onion rings and heat thoroughly. Fold in cheese or cheese soup and top with onion rings. Warm over very low heat until onions are hot, and serve at once. Six big servings.

Emmita's Sausage Skillet

Sometimes they are hard to find, but you can buy brown-and-serve sausages in an 8-ounce can. Or use fresh sausage when it's available.

eight-ounce brown-and-serve sausages or 1 pound sausage meat	1 ½ cups canned tomatoes
2 tablespoons chopped onion	2 cups cooked rice
	½ cup catsup or chili sauce

Brown meat with onion and drain off excess fat. Add other ingredients and simmer over low heat, tightly covered, for 30 minutes.

Pitch-and-Toss Tuna

You can make so many different dinner dishes by pitching a few tins into a pan and tossing the ingredients together! Brian and Liz Prydderch who live aboard *Tudor Rose*, like this with shell macaroni, tuna, and cream of mushroom soup. Emmita Weiher makes it with hominy grits. Vary it by using cream of asparagus soup too!

1 large can hominy grits or 2 cups cooked macaroni or spaghetti or rice	1 can cheddar cheese, cream of mushroom or cream of celery soup
1 can (six to eight ounces) tuna fish	

Mix all ingredients together and heat over low fire until well warmed. Fold in chopped hard-boiled eggs or drained mushrooms from a can, if desired. For a garnish, top with crushed cheese crackers or buttered bread crumbs. Serves 3 to 4 generously.

Tamed Chipped Beef on Toast

A few minutes of parboiling take the extra saltiness out of dried beef. Its light weight makes it a must for back-pack and canoe camping.

    4 ounces dried beef   ½ cup water
    1 can cream of mush-   ½ soup can milk or
      room soup   water
              1 tablespoon freeze-dried chives

Put dried beef in cold pan with water and bring to a boil. Drain. Add soup, water or milk, and chives and heat over low flame until warmed through. Spoon over toast, crackers, or potato sticks.

Hopping John

Poor in price but rich in food value. Give it a meatier taste by adding imitation bacon bits, and eat it as a main dish while you're waiting for your ship to come in. When it does, remember Hopping John for a side dish with grilled meats or as a hearty main dish with chunks of ham.

    3 cups cooked rice (1 cup
        raw rice)
    1 can black beans, black-eye peas
        or navy beans, with liquid
    2 tablespoons imitation bacon bits

Cook rice and stir in undrained can of beans. Heat thoroughly, season to taste, and stir in bacon bits before serving.

Chop-Chop Suey

Instant, because all the ingredients are cooked before you begin! A delicious, Chinese-y change from the usual meat-rice combinations and the crunchy noodles will wake up your taste.

1 pint home-canned beef, pork, veal or chicken or 2 cups cut-up meat from a can
1 can Chinese vegetables

soy sauce
1 can celery (optional)
1 tablespoon cornstarch
1 can Chinese noodles
2 tablespoons instant onion

Combine meat (with juices), undrained Chinese vegetables, celery, and instant onion in a saucepan. Add enough soy sauce to cornstarch to make a thin paste, then stir into other mixture as you stir over medium heat. Heat until smooth and thick, adding more liquid if necessary. Serve over Chinese noodles, with rice on the side.

Broiled Fish Deuteron

Nancy Royce Todd raved about this fish when we met in the Exumas. "I know it sounds strange, but try it," she begged. One bite converted her husband to a bitters fan.

4 servings any white fish

small onion minced
2 tablespoons bitters
butter

Melt a few tablespoons butter in a heavy skillet, and arrange fish in a single layer. Sprinkle with bitters and minced onion, then dot with more butter. Cover pan and bake over high heat 20-30 minutes or until fish flakes easily. Or, if you are broiling over an open fire or charcoal, broil on one side and then add onion, bitters and butter after turning.

White Clam Spaghetti

Phyllis and Don Streit are Bahamas "regulars" every season in their interesting English ketch, *Wooden World II* which still bears scars from its battering in the Dunkirk evacuation. This recipe and the next one are *Wooden World* stand-by's.

2 cans minced clams	grated Parmesan
1 tablespoon parsley	cheese
flakes	¼ cup butter
eight-ounce package	1 clove garlic or
spaghetti	equivalent
salt, pepper	

Drain clams, adding juice to water in which spaghetti is to be cooked. Put clams, parsley, garlic, and butter in a roomy pan or skillet and heat until bubbling. Then add grated cheese until the butter is absorbed and a thick paste is formed. Add cooked, drained, hot spaghetti and toss thoroughly until evenly coated with thick cream sauce. Salt and pepper to taste.

Wieners and Kraut

one-pound package hot	2 whole cloves
dogs or equivalent	apple, chopped, or
in canned hot dogs,	soaked dried apple
cocktail wieners, or	slices
Vienna sausages	pinch caraway seeds
2 one-pound cans	medium onion, chopped
sauerkraut	1 can beer

Drain kraut well and put in heavy saucepan with onion, apple, and spices. Cover with beer and simmer one hour. Add franks and heat through. If de-sired, quartered fresh potatoes can be simmered in the sauerkraut mixture, or canned potatoes can be added with the hot dogs.

8-Crew Stew

8	medium-size potatoes	2	twelve-ounce cans roast beef loaf
½	cup butter or oil		medium bottle ketchup
	salt, pepper		medium onion

Chop onion and fry in butter or oil until transparent and yellowed. Add potatoes and water to cover. Simmer until potatoes are tender. Then add meat in chunks, ketchup and seasoning, and simmer 20 minutes more. Serves 8 generously.

One-Pot Spaghetti

At last, a technique for cooking spaghetti with its sauce, instead of dirtying another pan. This recipe was worked out by Bob and Dana Sipeler, young Californians who lived aboard their 24-foot sloop, *Merry Myrtle.* For hearty eaters, plan one can of meatballs and gravy for each two servings.

8	ounces spaghetti	medium onion, chopped
1	can meat balls and gravy	sprinkling mixed Italian herbs
1	can tomato sauce	
	salt, pepper	

Break spaghetti into pressure cooker and nearly cover with water. Add remaining ingredients and bring up to full pressure. Cook under pressure for five minutes and remove from fire, to let pressure return to normal before removing cover.

Bully Beef Pie

No need to use a special pan for cooking instant mashed potatoes! Uku Walter, captain of the famous racing yawl, *Indigo*, worked out this recipe to use potato flakes or powder. In port, he uses fresh ground beef.

1 can onion soup   instant mashed
1 can corned beef,   potatoes as needed
    mashed   to thicken

Combine onion soup and mashed corned beef in a heavy saucepan and bring to a boil. Sprinkle potatoes over mixture, stirring constantly, until thick. Cover pan, remove from heat, and let stand at least ten minutes for flavors to blend. Taste before seasoning. The dish will probably need no salt, and the onion soup will provide a special tang. Turn out into casserole or baking dish, and crust the top with crushed crackers, deep-fried onions from a can, or buttered bread crumbs. Or, brown top by singeing quickly with a propane blowtorch!

Habibti *Casserole*

Frank and Roberta Fuqua designed and built their roomy cruising yawl, *Habibti*, in Egypt and live aboard as they travel Florida and the Bahamas.

4 onions, sliced   2 cups potatoes, diced
2 cloves garlic, minced   2 cups corned beef cut
¼ cup olive oil   in one-inch cubes
2 cups cut green beans   1 cup bouillon
                salt and pepper

Cook onions and garlic in the oil 2-3 minutes. Add potato and beef and cook five minutes. Add beans and bouillon. Bring to a boil, cover, simmer fifteen minutes, adding water if necessary. Season. Serves 4-6.

Jumble Aye-Aye!

A jambalaya that speed-steams in your pressure cooker to make use of seafood from a can, chunks of fresh crawfish, frozen shrimp when you have them. Open a one-pound tinned ham for breakfast and dice half of it into scrambled eggs. Save the other half for this 8-serving supper dish.

½ pound diced, cooked ham
garlic clove or equivalent
2 tablespoons salt
1 medium onion, coarsely chopped
dash pepper, cayenne, chili powder, and basil
one-pound can tomatoes
3 tablespoons fat

1 pound fresh shrimp, cleaned, or one crawfish tail, diced or 2 cans shrimp, rinsed and drained
fresh or dried green pepper
1 cup raw rice
⅛ teaspoon allspice
1 can mushrooms, drained

Sauté onion in fat in pressure cooker, then stir in rice until golden in color. Add remaining ingredients, (if using fresh garlic, mince well), close cover, and cook at full pressure for five minutes. Cool at once by dipping in cool water. Remove cover, stir, and cover again. Let stand five minutes, then serve. If you are on short water rations and cannot quick-cool pressure cooker, remove from fire until pressure is lost. Then stir, and serve at once.

Franks and Kraut

Eugene and Louise Villaret's *Ishmael*, like our own boat, sails without refrigeration, deep freeze, or oven.

Catsup and brown sugar in this recipe tame the sauerkraut and make it taste like a whole new vegetable!

½ onion, chopped or 2 tablespoons dried onion	2 tablespoons oil
	¾ cup water
	1 teaspoon prepared mustard
¾ cup catsup	1 pound franks or two cans Vienna sausages
1 tablespoon brown sugar	
1 can sauerkraut	

Sauté onion in oil and add catsup, water, sugar and mustard. Bring to a boil. Drain kraut and Vienna sausages, or slash franks, and add. Simmer over low fire for 20 minutes. Serve with boiled potatoes, or baked potatoes from the coals.

Shrimp Curry Ishmael

In port, Louise Villaret buys frozen shrimp soup and fresh sour cream for this curry. For cruising, she finds that tinned shrimp soup and packaged sour cream are excellent substitutes.

½ teaspoon curry powder	1 cup chopped onion
1 tablespoon butter	1 package sour cream mix, prepared according to directions
eight-ounce can shrimp	
1 can cream of shrimp soup	dash sherry

Pamper it in a double boiler, or in a heavy saucepan over very low heat or burner with tamer. Sauté onion in butter until soft and yellow. Add curry powder, shrimp, and soup, and heat through. Remove from heat and stir in sour cream, then sherry, if desired. Serve over rice, of course.

Apple Sizzle-wiches

Credit the Villarets, aboard *Ishmael*, for this hot lunch or light dinner. Make extra biscuits, English muffins or corn rounds for breakfast. Or use leftover pancakes or toast.

6 pieces bread, toast, or biscuit	1 teaspoon minced onion
sliced ham or Canadian bacon from a can	½ teaspoon salt
	½ cup catsup
mustard	1 teaspoon vinegar
1 tablespoon vinegar	1 teaspoon Worcestershire sauce
	large can pie-sliced apples

Arrange bread in bottom of heavy skillet with tight-fitting lid. Layer with sliced ham or Canadian bacon as desired, and spread with prepared mustard. Combine remaining ingredients in a saucepan and boil together for 10 minutes. Spoon over sandwiches in skillet, cover tightly, and cook over very low flame for 15 minutes. Remove to serving plate with pancake turner.

Giddyap Stew

Peter Helbrun, a Maine schoolteacher who sailed his 30-foot cutter, *Little Chance*, to the Windwards-Leewards during a sabbatical, took along a case of horsemeat! He's right, it is good, and it's pure meat, unlike many commercial canned products that are filled with gravies, cereals, tripe, and other stretchers. Hill's Horsemeat, chopped and cured in natural juices, is approved for human consumption by the U.S. Department of Agriculture, and makes a savory stand-in for chopped beef. Add tomato sauce, onions and spices for spaghetti sauce, and try it for other

chopped beef recipes too. You can plan three to four
big, meaty servings from every one-pound can.

1 can Hill's Horsemeat, chopped and cured	1 tablespoon olive oil
medium onion, sliced thin	medium onion, in chunks
1 can tomatoes	vegetables, as desired, for stew

Brown thin-sliced onion in olive oil, then add meat
and brown. Add onion chunks, tomatoes, and fresh
or canned vegetables as desired. Simmer until all
vegetables are tender.

Fish Stew Zucchini

Peter Helbrun, who has sailed many areas of the
world, also discovered that zucchini, canned in tomato sauce, makes an excellent base for fish stew.
Brown fish in butter or margarine first, then add potatoes or other vegetables as desired, the can of zucchini, and an extra tin of tomatoes. Another idea of
Helbrun's: boil fish in cheesecloth, and serve cold as
a salad with bottled dressing in your favorite flavor.

Egg Foo Yong

After eggs have been stored for a long period, the
yolks tend to break very easily. When you can no
longer cook them sunny side up, vary your omelette
and scrambled egg menu by serving this Chinese
treat.

6 eggs	one-pound can bean sprouts, drained
2 tablespoons instant onion	small can shrimp, tuna or crab
½ teaspoon pepper	1 tablespoon corn-starch
oil for frying	
1 tablespoon sugar	

1 ½ cups water	3 tablespoons soy
1 teaspoon salt	sauce

Beat eggs well and stir in onion, seasonings, bean sprouts, and fish. Heat oil in skillet and fry all at once, as an omelet, or individually in "pancakes." Serve with a sauce made by stirring soy sauce and water into cornstarch and sugar. Cook, stirring, until thick and smooth. Or, you may prefer to serve with beef gravy from a mix or a can, with a little soy sauce added.

Gourmet Casserole

To give a cooked-all-day taste to instant main dishes from package or can, begin with this wine "ash."

1 cup white wine	2 tablespoons
½ teaspoon thyme	freeze-dried
dash pepper	parsley
½ teaspoon salt	

Mix in the saucepan in which you will be combining your casserole, and boil for three minutes. Then play it by ear by adding canned chicken stew and a tin of peas, a jar of chicken and noodles, canned chicken à la king, a tin of boneless meat, or chicken plus rice or potato, and mixed vegetables. In short, use almost any casserole combination and your gourmet wine ash will transform it!

Sunup Supper

All of your work for this hot-weather dinner is done at breakfast time, when the day is still cool. Serve pancakes with syrup, and scrambled or three-minute eggs. Plan extra pancakes, and hard boil or scramble six extra eggs. Then, at sundown, make this dish with only the barest fire.

½ cup chopped onion	3 tablespoons
1 package sour	butter
cream mix	1 teaspoon
small can shrimp	garlic salt
pancakes	1 can cream of
6 eggs	asparagus soup

Sauté onion in butter until soft and yellow. Stir in garlic salt and undiluted soup. Fold in chopped hard-boiled or cup-up scrambled eggs and heat gently. Remove from heat and stir in sour cream, which has been prepared according to package directions, and shrimp. Heat pancakes over low fire in heavy, covered pan or skillet. Arrange on plates, and smother with shrimp mixture.

Barbecued Salmon

Jack Thompson of Monterey, California, does a lot of sailing in northern waters where fresh salmon are often caught for dinner. The secret for broiling this, and all fish, is a pair of grills. Buy a hamburger broiler or two large cake racks so broiling fish can be turned without disturbing.

1 fresh salmon, split
marinade made from 1 part soy sauce to 2
parts dry vermouth

Marinate fish two hours. Broil skin side down over hot coals, brushing occasionally with marinade, until fish starts to flake away from bone. Clasping two parts of grill together, turn fish and remove the part of the grill that is now on top. Skin will come away with grill. Broil about eight minutes more, brushing with marinade. Bone will lift out before serving.

DESSERTS

"How do you do it?" others will ask when you toss off these just-like-home confections without oven, broiler, electric mixer, blender, or the other kitchen conveniences. These recipes can be baked without an oven and skimp on eggs, which are often an expensive or unobtainable item away from "civilization."

Most popular among baking devices for boats and campers are stove-top ovens, some of them foldable. However, I find them too awkward and drafty, and hard to maintain at a high, even heat. Our oven is a heavy aluminum skillet with a heavy aluminum domed lid. It also doubles as our frying pan, griddle, and pan broiler. For baking, I use a metal rack (the one from our pressure cooker) on the bottom, set baking pans on it, and bake as in any other oven.

To bake at 350-375 degrees, preheat the covered skillet over high heat for ten minutes. Then place your cake or pie on the rack, cover tightly with the lid, reduce heat to a medium flame, and don't peek until at least three-fourths of the cooking time has passed. Then, open the lid just a crack every few minutes, to let steam escape.

Don't worry about guessing at your "oven" temperature. Your heavy skillet oven will keep an even heat in occasional wind gusts or stove flame-outs. Even during practice runs, I never had a cake fall or fail in this oven.

You'll see that most of these cake recipes don't call for a buttered pan. I find the results are the same

without buttering, if you're going to serve the cake
from the pan. Buy a small flexible spatula, the kind
used for spreading frosting, to cut and loosen cake
servings.

CAKES

Mayo Fudge Cake

No shortening to cream in this easy-on-the-arm cake.
For extra convenience, buy salad dressing in 8-
ounce jars.

2 cups flour	1 cup cold water
1 cup sugar	4 heaping teaspoons
2 teaspoons baking	cocoa
soda	1 cup salad dressing
2 teaspoons vanilla	(8-ounce jar)

Mix dry ingredients together well, right in an ungreased 8-inch square pan. Add salad dressing, water, and vanilla and work with spoon until smooth
and well blended, taking extra care to get any dry
ingredients out of the corners. Bake about 30 minutes at 350 degrees. Frost with confectioners' sugar
frosting, or:

Mock 7-Minute Frosting

Immediately after taking cake from oven, place 12
marshmallows in even rows on top. Let stand for a
few minutes until marshmallows are melty and
spreadable. Then swirl them to the sides of the cake
like frosting.

Po'-Boy Chocolate Cake

One of the cheapest cakes you can make, and certainly the simplest! Mix it right in the pan, without milk, butter, eggs, or shortening! For chewy brownies, use only half the water in the cake recipe, and add ½ cup chopped nuts.

1 ½ cups flour	1 teaspoon baking soda
3 tablespoons cocoa	1 teaspoon vanilla
1 cup sugar	5 tablespoons salad oil
1 teaspoon vinegar	1 cup cold water
½ teaspoon salt	

Mix dry ingredients well in an 8-inch square pan. With a spoon, make three holes in the mixture. Put the vanilla in one, the oil in the second, and the vinegar in the third. Pour 1 cup cold water over all, and work well with spoon, paying special attention to corners. Bake at 350 degrees for about 30 minutes or until cake tests done.

Crumb Cake

The topping bakes right on this moist, spicy German favorite. My husband remembers eating it warm from the oven at his grandmother's house after school. Mixing is made easier because you use a pastry blender.

2 cups flour	1 teaspoon nutmeg
1 teaspoon cloves	½ teaspoon salt
2 teaspoon cinnamon	¾ cup sour milk
½ cup shortening	(fresh, canned or
1 tablespoon molasses	nonfat dry milk
1 teaspoon baking soda	can be soured with
1 cup sugar	a few drops of
	vinegar)

1 egg

Mix dry ingredients except baking soda in a roomy bowl, then cut in shortening until the mixture is fine crumbs. Save ½ cup of the crumbs for topping. Mix beaten egg, molasses, sour milk, and baking soda. Quickly mix into the dry ingredients and stir thoroughly. Pour into an 8-inch square pan, sprinkle with crumbs, and bake about 30 minutes at 350 degrees.

Cookie Cake

In the roaming life, it is hardly practical to think in terms of layer cakes covered on three sides with sticky, sliding frostings. If your oven hasn't room for a pan large enough to hold a regular size cake mix, here is one way to use the two-layer mix in an 8-inch square pan. Frost, cut, and carry these chewy bar cookies right in the pan.

1 cake mix, any flavor (except angel food)	½ cup cooking oil 2 eggs 2 tablespoons water

Mix until well blended and pour into 8-inch square pan. Bake about 40 minutes, or until cake tests done, in a moderate, 350-degree oven.

Variations: add chopped nuts to a chocolate cake mix, to make brownies. Add a small package of chocolate chips and chopped nuts to white cake mix, to make chocolate chip "cookies". Add raisins and nuts to a spice cake mix for extra chewiness.

Everybody-Beat Frosting

For a very special occasion, bake two layers of any cake, then call in the crew by turn to tire their arms. This frosting takes an ocean of beating, but it's worth it to have such a delicious whipped-cream-like icing. We served it on a chocolate cake to celebrate a birthday party in a Fort Lauderdale boatyard.

1 cup milk	1 cup butter (as a
1 cup granulated	second choice, use
sugar	shortening, or
4 tablespoons instant-	margarine as a
blending flour	third choice)
1 teaspoon vanilla	

Mix milk and flour in a small saucepan and cook, stirring constantly, over very low heat. This will make a very thick paste. Set aside, covered, to cool completely. Beat sugar into butter very gradually and continue beating until mixture is smooth and has lost its grainy texture. Mix into it the cooled paste, then the vanilla. Beat thoroughly. This will frost the tops and sides of two layers generously.

Depression Cake

This is another cake that doesn't call for eggs. It is especially moist and spicy and takes well to a thin drizzling of confectioners' sugar frosting.

1 cup sugar	1 tablespoon fat (de-
1 cup raisins	pression-day recipes
2 cups flour	called for lard)
1 teaspoon nutmeg	2 teaspoons cinnamon
pinch salt	1 teaspoon baking
2 cups water	soda

Cook raisins and water together until they have simmered at a gentle boil for at least five minutes. Drain and add water if necessary to bring juice to 1 ½ cups. Remove from heat and add fat, stirring to melt. Then add dry ingredients which have been mixed or sifted together. Stir quickly but thoroughly and bake in 8-inch square pan at 350 degrees, 35 minutes or until cake tests done.

Honey Cake

Carry along a one-pound jar of honey especially for
this hearty, nourishing sweet. You'll use it all in the
cake and topping. No broiler to melt this topping to
a perfect, delicious glaze? Maybe you can stoke up
the coals to broil on this topping in a reflector oven.
Our secret? We blazed gingerly back and forth
across the topping with the propane blowtorch we
carry. Careful, though! Work quickly, evenly and
watchfully for even melting without burning.

1	cup uncooked oatmeal	2	eggs
1 ½	cups flour	1	cup boiling water
½	teaspoon salt	1	teaspoon baking soda
½	teaspoon ginger		
¼	teaspoon cloves	1	teaspoon cinnamon
¾	cup sugar	½	teaspoon nutmeg
½	cup shortening	1	cup honey

In a roomy bowl, cover shortening with oatmeal and
pour over them both the cup of boiling water. Let
stand 20 minutes. Add eggs and honey, then stir in
dry ingredients. Pour into 8-inch square pan and
bake in a 325-degree oven for an hour, or until cake
tests done. Spread topping mixture over top of
warm cake and broil until bubbly.

Topping:

¼	cup butter	⅓	cup honey
¾	cup chopped nuts	¼	cup flaked coconut

Cream butter and honey together, and mix in coconut and nuts.

Close-Haul Fruitcake

Sailing close-hauled is to sail as tight to the wind as
possible. This festive, fruity cake close-hauls your

budget by substituting packaged mincemeat for more expensive holiday fruits. For even stingier savings, more color, and a candy flavor children will love, substitute cut-up gumdrops for the nuts.

1 package mince- meat	2 ½ cups boiling water
1 cup shortening	1 ¾ cups sugar
	1 pound raisins

Mix and cook together 15 minutes. Then cool and add:

4 cups flour	2 teaspoons baking soda
1 teaspoon mixed spices (cinnamon, nutmeg, cloves)	1 cup nuts or chopped gumdrops
	½ teaspoon salt

Mix well and pour into a tube pan that will fit your oven or into tin cans or loaf pans. Bake 60 to 90 minutes in a slow oven, 300 degrees. Test for doneness with cake tester or toothpick. Makes one circular cake, or two loaves. Wrap in foil or rumsoaked cloth and let stand at least overnight before cutting. Like most fruitcakes, this one keeps for weeks.

Woodsman's Fruitcake

Far from city or shore, open a tin of your favorite fruit to make this moist puddinglike cake. Serve it warm with thick tinned cream.

1 cup sugar	1 cup flour
1 teaspoon baking soda	one-pound can any fruit, or fruit
1 egg	cocktail
1 teaspoon vanilla	½ cup brown sugar,
1 cup broken walnuts	firmly packed
	1 teaspoon salt

Mix sugar, flour, baking soda, and salt in an 8-inch square pan, 9-inch pie pan, or oven-proof baking dish. Stir in egg, vanilla, and can of fruit including all juice. Mix well, then sprinkle with brown sugar and walnuts. Bake about 45 minutes, or until bubbly, at 325 degrees.

Scrunch

Another pudding-cake that tosses together in seconds with a packaged one-layer cake mix. It was served to us in the anchorage at uninhabited, haunted Warderick Wells in the Exuma Cays by Lew and Nellwyn Foley of Houston, Texas, aboard *Sea Fever*. Try it with strawberries, peaches, rhubarb!

    one-pound can any fruit
    one-layer yellow cake mix
    2-3 tablespoons butter

Pour entire can of fruit, including juice, into 8-inch square pan. Sprinkle with dry cake mix and dot with butter. Bake at 375 degrees until top has browned. Spoon into sauce dishes and serve warm or cold with tinned cream or packaged whipped cream substitute. At home, try it with ice cream.

Carrot Cake

Carrots carry along beautifully without refrigeration, and will keep for several weeks if kept in a cool, dry place. You'll serve them raw, cooked—and in this colorful, vitamin-packed loaf cake!

2 cups sugar	3 cups flour
1 teaspoon baking soda	½ teaspoon salt
1 teaspoon cinnamon	2 cups coarsely grated carrots
	2 eggs

1 ⅓ cups salad oil   1 teaspoon vanilla
1 teaspoon lemon   ½ teaspoon almond
    extract   flavoring
              1 cup chopped nuts

Place a sturdy plastic bag in a medium-size mixing bowl and fold top down around edges to line bowl. (Experiment with different brands of bags until you find the sturdiest.) Combine sugar, flour, baking soda, salt, and cinnamon in bag. Then add oil and eggs. Remove top of plastic bag from bowl, grasp top, and work with hand until well mixed. Add flavorings and mix again. Then add carrots and nuts and work gently just until they are well distributed in batter. Squeeze out into greased and floured loaf pans, two large or three small size. Bake for one hour at 350 degrees. Turn out of pans and, while warm, glaze with lemon glaze:

Lemon Glaze
3 tablespoons lemon juice
3 tablespoons sugar

Mix together and drizzle over warm carrot cake. When cake has cooled, wrap tightly in foil or plastic wrap. Age overnight. Then slice into thin slices.

Apple-Y Crumb Cake

2 cups applesauce   ½ cup raisins
½ teaspoon cinnamon   ¼ cup butter
¼ teaspoon vanilla   2 cups graham
½ cup chopped   cracker crumbs
    almonds   ⅓ cup brown sugar

Plump raisins by covering with boiling water. Let stand ten minutes, then drain. Put 1 cup of the

graham cracker crumbs in a buttered 8-inch cake
pan or pie plate, cover with applesauce, and sprinkle
with vanilla, cinnamon, nuts, raisins, and brown
sugar. Top with remaining crumbs and dot with
butter. Bake 25 to 30 minutes in 350-degree oven.
Spoon into serving dishes and serve with vanilla
sauce:

Vanilla Sauce

2 cups milk	2 tablespoons
2 tablespoons sugar	cornstarch
1 egg	1 teaspoon vanilla

Combine in saucepan and stir well. Then cook over
low heat, stirring constantly, until thick and
smooth. Shortcut: in a shaker, combine 2 cups reconstituted nonfat dry milk and one package instant vanilla pudding mix. Shake vigorously one
minute and let stand until set. Or, sauce your
Crumb Cake with canned vanilla pudding.

Cornish Cider Cake

Use tinned apple juice or cider in this golden spice
cake from the coast of Cornwall. Then serve it
around the campfire or in the cockpit with hot cider
or hot buttered rum.

1 cup sugar	¼ cup flour
1 cup flour	1 cup butter
½ teaspoon allspice	1 teaspoon baking
2 cups cider or	powder
apple juice	2 eggs
1 cup golden raisins	1 cup currants
1 cup chopped nuts	

Cream butter and sugar, then beat in 1 cup of flour,
the baking powder, allspice, and eggs. Gradually

stir in cider. Shake nuts, raisins, and currants in a paper bag with the ¼ cup flour and stir into batter. Spread into a well-buttered deep 9-inch pan or, for easier removal, a spring form pan or tin cans. Bake one hour at 300 degrees. Cool for at least ten minutes in pan before turning out.

Schooner Prune Cake

On long cruises, we carry a case of those wonderful pitted prunes for baking, and especially for snatching straight and moist from the box. This cake will sell itself without trimming. Or serve it with a vanilla pudding sauce, fruit, or a dusting of confectioners' sugar icing.

½ cup cut-up pitted prunes, uncooked	½ teaspoon baking soda
½ cup boiling water	½ teaspoon cinnamon
½ teaspoon nutmeg	¼ teaspoon cloves
1 cup flour	¼ cup salad oil
¾ cup sugar	2 eggs
½ teaspoon salt	½ cup chopped nuts

Pour boiling water over prunes and let stand at least two hours. (I put the prunes to soak at breakfast time, when the water is boiling for coffee, to save lighting a fire later in the day.) Stir dry ingredients together in an 8-inch cake pan, then blend in remaining ingredients, including prune mixture. Stir well, paying special attention to corners. Bake 35-45 minutes at 350 degrees, or until cake tests done.

Pitchpole Cake

Bake it in your skillet, then turn it out onto a plate to show how prettily you have arranged the fruit on the bottom.

⅓ cup butter	½ cup brown sugar,
1 cup sugar	firmly packed
1 ⅓ cups flour	2 teaspoons baking
⅓ cup shortening	powder
1 teaspoon vanilla	½ teaspoon salt
Fruits, nuts, raisins,	⅔ cup milk
or jam	1 egg

Melt butter in heavy 10-inch skillet with tight-fitting lid. Arrange pieces of canned, drained fruits, nuts, raisins, or spots of jam in bottom of pan. Sprinkle with brown sugar. Make batter by creaming shortening with sugar. Add egg. Then add dry ingredients alternately with vanilla and milk. Beat until smooth, and pour over fruit pattern. Bake over medium flame, tightly covered, for 50 minutes or until cake tests done. Immediately turn out onto plate. Serve warm.

Floating Cake

As it bakes, this dessert floats a tender cake to the top as the sweet fruit sauce sinks. Your pastry blender saves creaming shortening into the batter. Canned pie filling also lessens preparation time.

1 cup any flavor fruit	dash salt
pie filling	2 tablespoons butter
1 cup flour	½ cup milk
2 teaspoons baking	1 cup boiling water
powder	1 teaspoon vanilla

½ cup sugar

Sift or mix dry ingredients in bowl and cut in butter with pastry blender. Add milk and vanilla, mix well, and spread into 8-inch square cake pan. Spoon pie filling over the top and pour the boiling water over all. Bake 40 minutes at 350 degrees. While warm, spoon into serving dishes, cake side down.

Left-over pie filling? Thin it with a little warm water to serve on pancakes the next morning.

Harvest Gingerbread

1 can pie-sliced apples or 1 package dried apples, soaked and cooked	dash nutmeg
	1 tablespoon melted butter
	¼ teaspoon cinnamon
small package gingerbread mix	2 tablespoons sugar

Prepare gingerbread mix according to directions and spread into 9 x 9 x 2-inch cake pan. Arrange apple slices or rings in rows and sprinkle with sugar and spices. Dot with butter and bake 30 minutes at 350 degrees. Serve in squares.

Cold Oven Cheesecake

No need to bake this lemon-y cake. And, if you're in areas where you can't buy cream cheese, leave it out. Your "cake" will still be firm, creamy, crusty, and re-markably like a true cheesecake!

1 cup cornflake crumbs	⅓ cup fresh or bottled lemon juice
½ teaspoon cinnamon	1 teaspoon vanilla or almond extract
2 tablespoons sugar	
⅓ cup butter, melted	eight-ounce package cream cheese
1 can (1 ⅓ cups) *condensed* milk (no substitutes)	one-pound can peaches, drained

Melt butter in 9-inch pie pan and stir in crumbs, sugar, and cinnamon until well blended. Reserve 2 tablespoons crumb mixture. Press remaining crumbs tightly around bottom and sides of pie pan.

If you have cream cheese, let it soften at room temperature and beat until fluffy. Blend in lemon juice, condensed milk, and vanilla or almond extract with egg beater and immediately turn into crust. If you are working without cream cheese, simply mix lemon juice and flavoring into condensed milk with egg beater until well blended and turn at once into pie shell. Arrange well-drained peaches on top and sprinkle with reserved crumbs. Let stand in shady place or in refrigerator or ice chest for at least an hour.

Jury-Rig Angel Food

A quickie dessert for beach cookouts or campfires and an excellent way to spirit away staling bread. Let the children bake their own over the coals on green pointed sticks.

two-inch cubes stale bread	fresh, canned, or packaged coconut
sweetened condensed milk	

Spear bread cubes securely on pointed sticks or skewers. Dip in milk then roll in coconut. Toast over open fire until coconut is evenly browned.

Nut-Cracker Sweets

Melty, calorie-crammed desserts baked in foil over the dying coals in your campfire or grill. Teach the children to assemble their own Sweets and to wrap them securely in foil.

For each Sweet:

2 graham crackers	⅓ of a milk chocolate
1 marshmallow	bar with almond

Make a sandwich from the two crackers with the chocolate and marshmallow between. Seal in individual squares of foil and roast, turning often, over coals until chocolate and marshmallows are melted. Stay away from flames and hot coals. Graham crackers burn easily!

Yukon Applesauce Cake

This spicy, moist cake and the next one are recipes that were given to us by Bob Leonard, a former Alaskan charter pilot. Neither recipe asks for eggs, which makes them especially popular in a state where eggs are dear.

1 cup brown sugar	2 teaspoons baking soda
½ cup butter	1 teaspoon cloves
1 teaspoon cinnamon	one-pound can applesauce
1 cup raisins	1 cup chopped nuts
2 ¼ cups flour	

Cream butter and sugar, then stir in dry ingredients with applesauce. Fold in raisins and nuts, and pour into angelfood cake pan or deep 8-inch square pan. (Fill pan only ⅔ full. Bake any leftover batter in cupcake tins or tin cans.) Bake 45 minutes or until cake tests done in 325-degree oven. Frost lightly or dust with confectioners' sugar.

Tomato Soup Cake

½ cup butter	½ cup chopped nuts, if desired
1 cup sugar	2 cups flour
1 teaspoon cinnamon	1 teaspoon nutmeg
1 can undiluted tomato soup	½ teaspoon salt
	1 cup raisins

Cream butter and sugar, then stir in dry ingredients alternately with tomato soup. Bake one hour at 325 degrees in 8-inch pan. (Fill pan only ⅔ full. Bake any leftover batter in cupcake tins or tin cans.)

Saucy Fudge Cake

Another eggless pastry, and a rich, gooey dessert that makes its own hot fudge sauce!

1	cup flour	2	teaspoons
¼	teaspoon salt		baking powder
2	tablespoons cocoa	½	cup milk
2	tablespoons	1	cup brown sugar,
	salad oil		firmly packed
4	tablespoons cocoa	1 ¾	cups boiling
¾	cup sugar		water

Bring water to boiling, then set kettle aside while you use fire to pre-heat oven. Mix flour, baking powder, sugar, salt, and 2 tablespoons of the cocoa in 8-inch square pan. Pour in milk and salad oil and mix well. Over this mixture, sprinkle the 4 tablespoons cocoa, then the cup of brown sugar. Pour the boiling water over all and bake 45 minutes at 350 degrees.

PIES

Anti-Roll Pie Crust

There is hardly room in the small galley to swing a cat, let alone a rolling pin. And yet the way to a captain's heart is inevitably through his pie tooth. There are many substitutes for traditional pie crust. This one, extremely buttery and tender, is closest to the pies I make on shore.

½ cup butter or
     margarine

1 cup plus 2 table-
    spoons flour
1 tablespoon sugar

Melt butter over low heat, right in the pie pan. Remove from heat. Add flour and sugar all at once and stir with fork until well blended. With fingers, press crust to bottom and sides of pie pan and form fluted edge. Bake as is for a pie shell, or proceed with custard or fruit fillings. This crust does bake and brown in a covered skillet or Dutch oven when set on a rack and baked at high heat.

For custard pie: prepare a package of custard mix (the kind with egg) according to package directions. Pour thin custard mixture into baked pie shell.

For fruit pies: empty a can of any flavor fruit pie filling into unbaked pie shell. Top with a crumb topping made by rubbing ½ cup flour and ¼ cup brown sugar into ¼ cup butter. Bake until crumb topping is slightly browned and edge of crust looks brown and flaky.

For fruit custard pies: into unbaked pie shell, place well-drained canned fruits, prepared dried apples, sliced fresh apples or thin-sliced fresh rhubarb. Sugar to taste. Pour over fruit a mixture of ¾ cup cream or evaporated milk, 3 tablespoons instant-blending flour, dash salt, dash cinnamon and ¼ cup sugar. Bake in pre-heated oven over high heat until custard is set and crust is browned.

For cream pies: bake pie shell in pre-heated oven at high heat until evenly browned. Cool and add cooked or instant puddings or canned pie fillings. Add coconut or bananas with vanilla pudding, if desired.

Nymph Errant *Key Lime Pie*

Annie Bolderson, aboard the schooner *Nymph Errant* in the Bahamas, wows her charter guests with this easiest version of a tropical classic. You'll find tiny, yellow juice-heavy key limes in native stalls and in most south-of-the-border ports.

2 cans sweetened condensed milk
juice of 6-12 key limes

With experience, you'll learn how much lime juice to add for exactly the tartness your family likes. Just a small amount of lime juice is enough to "set" the condensed milk. Keep adding the juice, blending in with an egg beater, until the mixture is tart to taste. Work quickly, because this filling firms up fast. Spread immediately into baked pie shell or crumb crust, and chill or set in shady place for at least an hour. Serve with whipped cream.

Coconut Pie Crust

3 tablespoons butter	1 ½ cups grated coconut (do not use shredded or flaked coconut or pie will be awkward to cut)
⅔ cup confectioners' sugar	
1 tablespoon milk	

Melt butter in pie tin over very low heat. Remove from flame and add milk, then confectioners sugar. Stir well, then blend in grated coconut and press to bottom and sides of pan. Let stand at least ten minutes before filling.

Soda Cracker Pie

More of a meringue than a pie, this Southern dessert is best served with whipped cream. Far from the

city, sauce it with warm melted preserves, canned
fruit, or vanilla pudding from a tin.

1 cup sugar	12 saltines, rolled
1 teaspoon almond	fine
flavor	1 cup broken
¼ teaspoon cream	pecans or cut-up
of tartar	dates
3 egg whites	

Grease a 9-inch ovenproof pie pan with oil only. Beat
egg whites with the cream of tartar until stiff. Add
sugar very gradually. Fold in saltines, flavoring, and
nuts or dates. Bake 20-25 minutes at 350 degrees.
Cool and cut into wedges.

Chocolate Crust

¼ cup soft	2 envelopes pre-
butter	melted choco-
1 cup graham cracker	late
crumbs	1 cup confectioners'
1 tablespoon water	sugar

Mix well in 8- or 9-inch pie pan with a fork, then
press mixture firmly to bottom and sides of pan.
Chill if possible, or let stand in cool place for an hour.
Fill.

Cookie Crust

When your cookies lose their snap in outside air,
give them a second life as pie crust. I made a small
zippered bag from heavy duck, and put all stale and
leftover cookies into it. Then, instead of rolling them
into crumbs with a rolling pin, I roll the bag with a
bottle or pound with the flat edge of a hammer until

crumbs are fine. Then it's a simple, mess-free matter
to pour the crumbs directly into the pie pan.

> 1 ½ cups any kind of crumbs or mixture of
> crumbs (vanilla wafers, graham crackers, soda
> crackers, ginger snaps, chocolate cookies,
> cereal crumbs, etc.)
> 3 tablespoons butter
> 1 tablespoon sugar

Over very low heat, warm butter in pie pan until
melted. Remove from heat and stir in crumbs and
sugar with fork until evenly blended with butter.
Press to bottom and sides of pie pan. Bake for ten
minutes in a hot oven, or fill without baking.

Pecan Pie

One of the most sugary of desserts and lucky for you
because nutrition-rich nuts carry forever in your
lockers. There isn't room in my galley to carry corn
syrup, a seldom-used item that is called for in most
pecan pie recipes. That's why this recipe best fills the
bill on board for us.

one recipe anti-roll pie crust, pressed into 9" pie pan

4 eggs	2 cups brown sugar,
1 cup sugar	firmly packed
¼ cup butter	¾ cup water
	1 teaspoon vanilla

enough pecan halves to cover bottom of lined pie pan

In a large mixing bowl, beat eggs with hand beater
until light and frothy. Set aside and bring sugars and
water to a rolling boil in a thick saucepan. Boil
three minutes and then stir hot syrup gradually into
eggs. Blend in softened butter and vanilla. Turn into
unbaked pie shell on which pecan halves have been
arranged. They will rise to the top, candy coated,

during baking. Bake at 350 degrees for an hour, or until custard is just set. Cool before cutting.

COOKIES

In tiny camp ovens and without special space-stealing cookie sheets, it takes too long to make homestyle cookies. Concentrate instead on bar cookies, cooked in one pan and cut into portions to stock your cookie jar.

Scotch Squares

¼ cup salad oil	1 cup brown sugar,
1 egg	firmly packed
¼ teaspoon salt	1 cup flour
1 cup coarsely broken nuts	½ teaspoon vanilla

Blend oil and sugar in a medium-size mixing bowl, then add egg and mix well. Stir in flour and salt, vanilla, and nuts. Spread in ungreased 8-inch square pan and bake 30 minutes at 350 degrees. Cool five minutes then cut in squares. Loosen and lift from pan with small frosting spatula and cool completely before storing in airtight jar.

Sandbars

1 cup butter	½ cup plus 2 table-
2½ cups flour	spoons sugar

Cream butter and sugar together until smooth, then work in flour. Dough will be very stiff. Spread in 8-

inch square pan, taking care to make dough an even depth in all spots. Score shallowly with a knife into 16 squares. Bake at 350 degrees for 35-40 minutes or until cookies are lightly browned. Cut while warm and remove from pan while cool.

Fry Cook Cookies

½ cup butter	1 ½ cups graham cracker crumbs
1 cup chopped nut-meats	fifteen-ounce can condensed milk
three-and-a-half-ounce can flaked coconut	six-ounce package chocolate chips

Melt butter over low heat in heavy 10-inch skillet, preferably aluminum. Remove from heat and add remaining ingredients one by one, in layers. Drizzle sweetened condensed milk over all. Cover tightly and bake over low flame for 25 minutes or until cookies test done. Cool, uncovered, 15 minutes before cutting. Then cut into wedges or squares and remove carefully from pan with thin flexible spatula.

Coral Reefs

½ cup butter	½ teaspoon vanilla
32 marshmallows	5 cups Rice Crispies

Cook butter and marshmallows over low flame until thick and syrupy. Remove from heat and add vanilla. Pour mixture over Rice Crispies in large, buttered bowl. Toss until evenly coated. Press into buttered pans or dishes and let stand several hours. Cut into squares.

Cocoa Logs

1 cup chocolate chips (six-ounce package)	4 cups ready-to-eat chocolate flavored cereal
⅓ cup peanut butter	

Melt chocolate bits in a heavy saucepan over very low heat. Add peanut butter, stirring constantly, until well blended. Add cereal and mix until well coated. Press into buttered pans or dishes. Cool and cut into logs.

Kettle Cookies

Yes, you boil them!

1 cup sugar	¼ cup butter
¼ cup plus 2 table-spoons milk	1 ½ cups quick oats
	⅓ cup coconut
1 teaspoon vanilla	38 pecan halves
⅓ cup chopped nuts	

Shake oats, coconut, and chopped nuts together in a bag. Set aside. In heavy saucepan, heat sugar, butter, and milk to boiling and boil three minutes. Remove from heat. Quickly add vanilla and mixture of dry ingredients and stir until thoroughly mixed. Drop by teaspoons onto waxed paper or foil and top with pecan halves. Dry several hours before storing.

Brownies

Stir up these rich, fudgy brownies with either cocoa or baking chocolate.

¾ cup flour	½ teaspoon baking powder
6 tablespoons cocoa or two packets pre-melted chocolate	½ cup nuts
	2 eggs
½ teaspoon salt	1 teaspoon vanilla
½ cup butter	1 cup sugar

Cream butter and sugar together, and add eggs one at a time. Then add baking powder and cocoa and mix. Add flour and salt and mix again, then add vanilla and nuts. Spread into 8-inch square pan and bake 30-35 minutes, or until testing done, at 350 degrees.

Rum Dums

Nutty nuggets that never see an oven! A must for the West Indies, and a holiday treat up north.

twelve-ounce box vanilla wafers, crushed	2 tablespoons cocoa few drops imitation butter flavoring
1 cup sifted confectioners' sugar (plus more for rolling cookies)	¼ cup dark West Indies rum 3 tablespoons honey 1 cup chopped pecans

Mix dry ingredients well, then blend in honey and rum. Form into one-inch balls and roll in confectioners' sugar. Store in tightly-covered coffee tins or plastic boxes. Better still, store them in a coffee tin that hasn't been washed. The few remaining crumbs of coffee will lend an even more special flavor!

OTHER DESSERTS

Crêpes Chocolat

Because they are pancakes, they are easy for your travels. Because they have a lovely French name, they make tonight a special occasion.

1 packet pre-melted chocolate	2 eggs
¼ cup sugar	1 teaspoon salt
¼ teaspoon cinnamon	1 cup water
½ cup cream or evaporated milk	confectioners' sugar
	¾ cup flour
	jam
butter	

Beat eggs until thick and lemon colored. Beat in sugar and salt very gradually, then blend in chocolate and cinnamon. Combine water and cream or milk, and add alternately with flour. Heat griddle or heavy skillet well and oil evenly. Pour 2 tablespoons batter at a time and cook as for pancakes, turning once. As each is removed, put a tablespoon of jam into the center and roll tightly. Serve with prepared fudge sauce and a sprinkling of confectioners' sugar.

Taffy Pull

More than a dessert! It's an after-supper sport for the whole family. Any number can play, even the tots.

1 ½ cups mild-flavor molasses	¾ cup sugar
2 tablespoons butter	2 teaspoons vinegar
1 teaspoon flavoring (vanilla, lemon, orange, pineapple)	

Bring molasses, sugar, butter and vinegar slowly to a boil, stirring constantly. Boil 25-30 minutes, stirring constantly during last minutes of cooking time and test to see if a small amount dropped in cold water will form a hard ball. (260 degrees if you have a candy thermometer.)

Remove from heat and stir in flavoring, then pour

taffy onto aluminum foil to cool. When you can dent it with your finger, it should be cool enough to work. Divide into lumps for each person, and give everyone butter to rub on their hands. Then everybody pull and stretch and squeeze until the candy turns a light golden yellow. Draw out into long strips and cut with scissors into inch-long lengths. Eat it up, or wrap each piece in a twist of waxed paper.

Fake Flan

Amazing! To make a rich caramel custard, simply remove the paper label and top from a can of sweetened condensed (not evaporated) milk. Cover securely with aluminum foil, and place in about an inch of water in your pressure cooker. Cook at full pressure for 30 minutes, preferably over your breakfast fire so it has time to cool thoroughly before lunch or dinner.

When cool, remove bottom of can, loosen custard around edges, and turn out onto cutting board or plate. Cut into 4 or 5 slices. Flan will be firm, and rimmed with luscious brown caramel. Because this dessert is so rich and sweet, you may prefer to serve it with fruit, whipped cream, milk, or cold cream from a tin.

SAUCES AND TOPPINGS

Cranberry Sauce

one-pound can whole cranberry sauce
¼ cup rum

Combine in saucepan and bring to a boil. Serve over plain cakes or puddings.

Cherry Sauce

twelve-ounce jar cherry preserves
2 tablespoons Kirsch

Combine in small saucepan and bring just to a boil. Serve over instant vanilla pudding or custard pie.

Mincemeat Sauce

1 ⅓ cups ready-to-use mincemeat
¼ cup rum

Bring to a boil in small saucepan and remove from heat. Serve over spice cake, pound cake or gingerbread.

Tosca Topping

2 tablespoons butter
¼ cup chopped almonds
1 tablespoon instant-blending flour
¼ cup sugar
2 ¼ tablespoons milk

Melt butter in small saucepan or skillet. Stir in other ingredients and let come to a boil. Spread on top of a warm cake and return to oven for 10 to 12 minutes, or until topping is glossy.

Chocolate Sauce

1 can sweetened condensed milk
½ teaspoon vanilla
few drops butter or rum flavor
2-3 tablespoons cocoa or 1-2 packets pre-melted baking chocolate

Mix thoroughly and serve over plain white cake,
packaged lady fingers, stale brownies, ice cream, or
custard.

Fruit Cream

½ can sweetened condensed milk (⅔ cup)	3 tablespoons lemon juice (fresh or bottled)
1 cup cut-up canned fruit (small can)	Fruit juice or water

Mix lemon juice into condensed milk with spoon or
rotary beater, until thickened. Fold in fruit (crushed
pineapple, cut-up peaches, fresh bananas, blueberries, etc.). Thin with water or juice from canned
fruit until sauce is thinned to desired consistency.
Serve with gingerbread, plain white cake, or with
fruit cake or plum pudding from a can.

Wine Foam

Plenty work and plenty worth it, when you spoon this
hot, heavenly sauce over warmed plum pudding or
spicy apple pancakes for a Sunday night supper.
For the real thing, detour through Deidesheim
during your next camping trip into Germany, and
order apple fritters with wine sauce at the 700-year-
old Die Kanne.

8 eggs ½ cup white wine pinch salt	1 cup confectioners' sugar

In a heavy saucepan or double boiler, over low heat
beat egg yolks and sugar until thick and foamy. Add
salt and wine, and continue beating (with spoon,
whisk or rotary beater) until thick and foamy.

Remove from heat and fold in stiffly-beaten egg whites.

SANDWICHES AND SNACKS

A daily selection of sandwiches can be a real challenge for the cruising homemaker when store-bought bread isn't handy. These recipes were chosen especially for use with breads other than the traditional sandwich loaf.

Spread peanut butter with jelly, honey, crisp bacon bits, sliced sweet pickle, sliced banana or applesauce, on Boston brown bread from a can.

Mash sardines, moisten with a little lemon juice, and spread on saltines, then sprinkle with grated cheese.

Mash corned beef from a can and moisten with grated onion and chili sauce, to spread on Swedish hardtack (rye crackers.)

Lavish slices of canned Boston brown bread with cold baked beans and layer with thin coins sliced from canned Vienna sausages. Crown with a tiny hill of sweet relish.

Bake extra corn muffins at breakfast time. At lunch, split the cold leftovers, spread them with chili con carne from a can, and dust with grated onion.

Smooth pineapple-cheese spread from a jar onto crisp round crackers, and sprinkle with salted peanuts.

Split leftover breakfast biscuits and butter well, then sandwich in asparagus spears from a can. Sauce with a can of cheddar cheese soup, heated well.

Carry cans of date and nut bread, to slice thin and spread with pimiento cheese spread from a jar.

HAPPY HOUR

Even after the ice is gone, cooling and delicious drinks can be made by combining juices and powders you'll find on the market. Most of the cruising people we meet have turned to rum, because it somehow seems the most natural drink without ice.

Use ready-mix powders for whiskey sours, daquiri's, etc. and add extra water to taste to make up for the missing ice.

Helen and Bob Williams, aboard *Zlatka*, like gin and grape Kool-Aid.

Wally Johnson, aboard *Royal Star,* mixes rum with a lemon or lime-flavored iced-tea mix and water.

Laura and Don Mintz, aboard *Capella* out of New York City, carry envelopes of a pineapple-grapefruit drink mix. It tastes remarkably like fresh juice and makes a delicious rum punch even without ice.

Bill Sparks, aboard *Roulette*, likes white rum mixed with red fruit punch from a can.

Bill Wright, manager of Hawk's Nest Creek Marina at Cat Island, makes a rum punch dubbed Hawk's Nest Milk. Concoct your own combination of rum, fruit juice, and a splash of soda if you have it. Then add a dash of Bill's secret spicer, Tia Maria liqueur.

Make a cooling spritzer by combining your favorite wine half and half with club soda.

Experiment with coconut milk in punches.

Open a tin of tomato juice to make a Bloody Mary with gin or vodka, Tabasco, Worcestershire and a dash of salt.

Make a passable Screwdriver with orange breakfast drink from a powder, gin or vodka.

Canned grapefruit juice makes a Salty Dog, with gin or vodka and a pinch of salt.

Orange, lime, lemon, or orange-pineapple flavored gelatine dessert mixes make a fruity mixer for drinks you are not serving iced. Dissolve the powder in a cup of boiling water, then add 2 cups cool water and allow to cool to room temperature before mixing with liquor. More exotic: a Cranbreaker made from cranberry gelatine.

Make a cool lager seem cooler by squeezing in half a lime.

Rum Squash

In the Windward-Leeward Islands, they are called lemons (pronounced lemoans). In the Bahamas, they are called sours or sour oranges. They look like pale oranges with the hives. Single-hander Peter Helbrun, aboard *Little Chance,* recommends them with rum.

sour oranges	sugar to taste
water	ice, if possible

Squeeze half a sour into glass and add sugar to taste. (Tastes vary and so do sours, so take a trial sip.) Add a jigger of rum and a twist of peel, then fill glass with water and ice. This drink can be served iced or not, long or short.

Sangria

1 bottle (about 1 ½ pints) Spanish red wine	1 lemon, sliced thin
	2 oz. Cointreau
2 tablespoons sugar	twelve-ounce bottle club soda
½ orange, sliced thin	2 ounces brandy or Grand Marnier
1 ½ trays ice cubes or equivalent in water or soda	

Combine everything except soda and ice in a large pitcher or shaker and stir until sugar is dissolved. Let stand 20 minutes, then add soda and ice and serve in tall glasses.

Hijacker

¼ cup gin	¼ cup white rum
1 tablespoon lemon juice	¼ teaspoon grenadine syrup

Serve over crushed ice, if possible. If not, fill glass with cool water.

Hot Buttered Rum

Tove and Ole Arnfast rustled up this steaming, buttery bracer on a frosty October night in Fort Lauderdale, aboard their trimaran, *Kattegat*. This is our closest approximation of their guess-and-by-gosh technique.

¼	pound butter	1	teaspoon cinnamon
¼	teaspoon nutmeg	¼	teaspoon cloves
⅓	cup brown sugar, firmly packed		

Soften butter at room temperature and work in sugar and spices with back of a spoon. Into each mug, place a jigger of dark rum. Fill with boiling water and stir in a teaspoon of the butter mixture.

Yellow Bird

Chris and Chuck Grey, aboard *Altair III*, serve this tropical specialty from their blender. Here is how I make it in a one-quart shaker:

1	can frozen orange-grapefruit juice concentrate or substitute canned orange and grapefruit juices	1	cup rum
		½	cup banana liqueur

Fill shaker with water and ice, shake, and serve over more ice with a slice of fresh lime.

Coffee Drambuie

Aboard *Tudor Rose* in Yacht Haven, Nassau, Brian Prydderch serves after-dinner coffee hot, black, and with a shot of Drambuie liqueur in each full-sized cup.

Pickled Conch

Even first-timers in tropic waters can find and dive for conch. We wore out our stock of conch recipes before we learned to spear crawfish and grouper. This very different conch treatment is from Eugene and Louise Villaret, aboard *Ishmael,* who serve it with cocktails.

hammered conchs, cut into strips	vinegar
lime juice	pickling spices
	onion chunks

Clean and pound conch before cutting into strips. Then sprinkle with juice of one lime, or a few tablespoons of bottled lime juice. Cover with vinegar, sprinkle with pickling spices and mix in onion chunks. Allow to sit overnight, then drain and serve.

Nymph Phritters

Annie Bolderson, aboard *Nymph Errant,* discovered this easiest of ways to make cocktail tidbits from leftover dolphin, fruits, vegetables, or crawfish catches that weren't large enough to feed the whole crew. Let your imagination run wild when you start dipping. Cauliflower, pineapple chunks, bananas, fresh shrimp, cut-up crawfish!

pancake mix	beer
drained, cut-up fruits, fish, etc.	oil for deep frying

Add beer to pancake mix and stir, adding more beer until you have a thick batter. Heat oil, at least three inches thick, in a heavy saucepan to 375 degrees, or until a test drop of batter sizzles immediately when dropped in. Dip tidbits into batter to coat completely, then deep fry until crisp and golden. Remove to drain on paper towel. These tidbits should be served hot.

Seviche

Marinate your morning catch all day, to serve at cocktail time.

2 pounds white fish fillets	½ cup lime juice
½ cup lemon juice	1 tablespoon catsup

Cut fish into tidbit-size strips or chunks and marinate all day or overnight in other ingredients.

Barbecue

½ cup catsup	1 tablespoon molasses
1 teaspoon prepared mustard	canned lunchmeat

Heat catsup, molasses, and mustard gently until blended and bubbly. Cut luncheon meat in half-inch cubes and heat thoroughly in sauce. Spear with toothpicks and serve hot.

Cocktail Croutons

A spicy, tasty way to use stale bread or leftover biscuits. This is a "must" recipe for us in the tropics, where homemade bread, and bread from island bakeries, molds within three days.

stale bread, cut in inch-size cubes
Salad Supreme seasoning
butter

Heat several tablespoons butter in a heavy skillet and stir in bread cubes, tossing to coat evenly. Add more butter if necessary. Sprinkle with seasoning and continue cooking, tossing constantly, until brown and crisp. Serve in a bowl, for finger food.

INDEX